OUACHITA TRAIL
GUIDE #5

TIM ER

TIM ERNST PUBLISHING

JASPER, ARKANSAS

WWW.TIMERNST.COM

The cover photo is of Forked Mountain in the Flatside Wilderness Area.

Library of Congress Control Number: 00-191507
ISBN 13: 9781882906437
Printed in the USA

This guidebook was produced in cooperation with
the United States Forest Service
Arkansas State Parks
and Friends of the Ouachita Trail (FoOT) Volunteers

Other books by Tim Ernst:

Arkansas Hiking Trails guidebook
Arkansas Dayhikes guidebook
Arkansas Waterfalls guidebook
Arkansas Nature Lovers guidebook
Buffalo River Hiking Trails guidebook
Ozark Highlands Trail guidebook
Arkansas Portfolio picture book
Wilderness Reflections picture book
Buffalo River Wilderness picture book
Arkansas Spring picture book
Arkansas Wilderness picture book
Arkansas Portfolio II picture book
Buffalo River Dreams picture book
Arkansas Waterfalls picture book
Arkansas Landscapes picture book
Arkansas Wildlife picture book
Arkansas Autumn picture book
Arkansas Portfolio III picture book
Arkansas Landscapes II picture book
Arkansas Nightscapes picture book
Buffalo River Beauty picture book
A Rare Quality Of Light picture book
Arkansas In My Own Backyard picture book
Arkansas Beauty picture book
Arkansas Splendor picture book
Arkansas Greatest Hits picture book
The Search For Haley
The Cloudland Journal ~ Book One & Two

www.TimErnst.com

FOREWORD

Walden Pond had David Thoreau. The Sierra Nevadas had John Muir. The Appalachian Trail had Benton MacKaye. The Ozark Highlands Trail has Tim Ernst.

Always on the move, Tim wasn't satisfied to be the father, midwife, and grandfather of the Ozark Highlands Trail. He came down to explore the unique qualities of the Ouachita National Recreation Trail too. The result is in your hands: the *Ouachita Trail Guide*.

This 223-mile trail from Talimena State Park in Oklahoma to Pinnacle Mountain State Park near Little Rock, Arkansas, has as many challenges and downright hard places as it has beautiful streams and vistas.

Unlike the Ozark Highlands Trail, which goes up and down all day long, the Ouachita Trail will climb to a hogback ridge, and stay there for hours. So knowing where the water is (or is supposed to be), and when the springs and creeks are dry, can make a hike one to remember, or one you would like to forget!

There is much to see and enjoy on the Ouachita Trail, but there are also real life dangers, and a few "tricky situations," especially for the novice backpacker. For example, there are some months only a fool would get out on the trail.

I guess I've hiked about 1,000 miles with Tim, and shared more campfires than either of us can remember. As far as I'm concerned, there is no one better qualified to write this Guide, and to help you appreciate and enjoy the Ouachita Trail.

If you pay attention to Tim in this Guide, you can save yourself much grief, and really have a great hike!

Happy Trails,

Jim Rawlins

Jim Rawlins

(Jim is the grandfather of the Ouachita Trail, wrote the original guidebook to it, and is one of the most knowledgeable outdoorsmen in the country.)

TABLE OF CONTENTS

INTRODUCTION

Welcome to this revised edition of the *OUACHITA TRAIL GUIDE*. What you have in your hands is the best resource available for hiking or biking this great trail. With this book in your pack, you are certain to enjoy the Ouachita Trail (OT).

The first thing that you need to do is to read all of this introduction. Once you've waded through it, you'll be ready to plan your hike and head to the woods. The book is designed to be easy to navigate through. There is a quick reference map on the back cover that shows the trail broken down by the ten sections, and what page the map and description for that section are on. At the top of each page are mile points described on that page.

It would also be helpful to re-read each individual section before you hike it, just in case you need to know something in advance, like that you should have stashed water somewhere because there was none on the trail. It is also good to read about the day's hike each morning, so that you can be alert to what is ahead.

This book was written by a hiker, for hikers, in a first-person format. The descriptions in this book were edited down from tapes that I made while hiking the trail. Although I have hiked the OT many times during the past 33 years, the main commentary was taken from a single end-to-end hike that I made in March of 1993 (major updates in 2012).

***Since I first wrote this guidebook, more than half of the OT has been opened up to mountain bike use. I must admit I was against this at first, but now I feel like it was a good idea and support their efforts. The various mountain bike clubs and retail shops in the area are good folks to work with, pull their own weight (and then some) as far as trail maintenance goes, and are good stewards of the trail. While I own three mountain bikes myself, I am not an expert biker, have never biked on the OT, and have not written the descriptions in this guidebook with mountain bikes in mind. Obviously the mileages, maps, and descriptions are the same no matter if you are on foot or rubber, and I expect everyone who uses this great trail will have a grand time!

My goal was to put something in your hands that was as close as I could get to a real person standing there giving you information, leading you by the hand. In the process, the "flavor" of my speech was retained—sorry about that. I think that I even invented a word or two.

I try to point out as many special scenic spots (SSS's) as I can, but I don't pretend to tell you about every wonderful place there is. In fact, I'm sure that there are many times more SSS's along the way than I tell you about. You'll just have to discover all the rest on your own.

There is a map and narrative description included for each of the ten trail sections. I don't take my information from what others have said or written, or guess about such things as mileage. I push a measuring wheel and carry a tape recorder while I hike, and the information presented here is as accurate as I know how to produce.

There is a great deal of information in this introduction that deals with other stuff, like the weather, bugs, camping, water, low impact use, etc., that I hoped you would find useful. Of course, all the reading in the world won't help if you don't get out and kick up a little dust, so I hope that you are able to use this book and do some hiking.

HISTORY OF THE OUACHITA TRAIL

The OT is a National Recreation Trail, 223 miles long, and runs from Talimena State Park in Oklahoma, through the heart of the Ouachita National Forest, to Pinnacle Mountain State Park just outside of Little Rock, Arkansas.

The OT was built from 1971–1981 by various Forest Service and State Park programs and groups of young folks. It was the first long-distance hiking trail in this part of the country, and the longest.

The trail has had a bad reputation in the past, fueled by various articles by some who have hiked it. And I must say that the reputation was fairly accurate. Much of the trail was a mess because of lack of use and maintenance, and a lot of it was built on poor locations to begin with. Terry Keefe of Little Rock was the first person I knew to hike the entire trail, and he found it (when he could) nearly impassable in spots.

When Jim Rawlins published his classic guide to the OT in 1985, the Forest Service realized that the trail was in terrible shape, and decided to do something about it. With that came a new wave of managers to implement some of the much-needed improvements. The picture is not totally rosy now, but things are considerably better than they ever have been, and getting more so each year. The Forest Service is committed to improving all aspects of the OT, and continues to do so.

One of those improvements was to implement a protected trail corridor, 200 feet on either side of the trail, that is basically managed as a linear park (i.e., no clear-cuts). Since the trail was often devastated by clear-cuts, this was a major step.

Trailheads were added at important access points. The entire trail was signed and blazed so that it could be found and followed. The Forest Service actually started *asking* for input from the using public. And now they have established a system of hiker shelters along the trail.

During the winter of 2000 a devastating ice storm literally wiped out a large portion of the OT. It took many months and even years for forest service personnel, contracted workers, and volunteers to get the trail back open again. Out of all this mess a group of incredible and dedicated volunteers were formed and charged themselves with the continued maintenance and upkeep of the entire OT. Calling themselves "Friends of the Ouachita Trail" (FoOT), they have put together a wonderful group of volunteers that now adopt and maintain the trail from one end to the other, and maintain a web page with regular trail condition updates. You can learn more about this group—and join their efforts—by taking a look at page 131.

The OT has come a long way baby. But it still has a long way to go. It will get there a lot faster with your help. Volunteers are always needed for trail maintenance, as well as other activities. If you enjoy this trail, you should join FoOT and contribute some time to keeping it in good shape. Contact any of the Forest Service offices (see page 132) or FoOT for more info.

OUACHITA NATIONAL FOREST

This is the oldest and largest National Forest in the South. It was established in 1907 and contains 1.6 million acres in Arkansas and Oklahoma. It is mainly a pine forest, with lots of hardwoods too.

Most of the Ouachita Trail is on the Ouachita Forest, and is managed by their Ranger Districts. I mention which District manages each section at the beginning to that section. The Forest Supervisor's Headquarters is in Hot Springs, Arkansas. See page 132 for the address and telephone numbers of all their offices.

The Forest Service personnel are aggressively trying to upgrade the OT and make it one of the best trails in the United States. From the Supervisor of the Forest to the technician in the field, they are dedicated to this trail project. They helped me a great deal with this guidebook, and are anxious to work with the public on trail issues. They welcome your comments and suggestions. Feel free to drop by any of their offices, or flag one of them down in the field and say "hi."

The Ouachita National Forest is a *working* forest. It is not a National Park. Don't get too upset if you see forest management practices going on, including timber sales and gas pipelines. These are simply part of the whole picture, as is recreation. You should not see timber sales within the protected trail corridor though—200 feet on either side of it. If you do, contact the Forest Service, because either someone has made a mistake, or the land is actually private and just comes close to the trail.

STATE PARKS

There is a State Park on either end of the trail, Talimena and Pinnacle Mountain, as well as one along the trail, Queen Wilhelmina. Each park has its own special features and facilities, and their own way of doing things. Of special note is the incredible view from Queen Wilhelmina, which is located on top of Talimena Scenic Drive, and the vast array of interpretive programs that Pinnacle Mtn. provides.

If you are leaving your vehicle at any of these parks, be sure to

7

check in with their office to let them know what you are doing. Talimena and Queen Wilhelmina have full RV hookups, as well as *showers* and campsites. The camping areas may be closed during the dead of winter though, so be sure to call ahead. There is no camping at Pinnacle Mtn. (but there is a campground nearby). All three parks have personnel on duty all year.

TRAIL MARKERS

The Ouachita Trail is blazed with a standard 2" x 6" blue paint blaze. Since blue is my favorite color, I really like them (most other trails that intersect with the OT and spur trails are blazed with white paint). There are a few spots here and there that could use a few more blazes, but overall the trail is pretty well marked the entire length. If you see two blazes, or one or two tilted left or right, then there is an intersection or confusing turn close, so be alert. Also at many of the intersections there may be a blue-blazed "OT" symbol or other type of marker—like the one pictured on the tree inside the front cover of this guide. Look for these and hike towards them at intersections if you see them, although they are being phased out and may be faded.

If you simply can't find any blazes to follow, and you think that you are still on the trail, try to use some common sense and look for the *trail tread* or corridor route through the woods, not necessarily for blazes. (Hiking blaze-to-blaze is not much fun anyway since you miss all the good stuff around you!) Also look for clues like cut branches, rocks lined up in a row, and other signs of man that show the way. If you follow along with my description, and stay alert, you shouldn't have any problems following the trail.

MAPS, MILEAGES AND ELEVATION PROFILES

All of the maps in this book were created on computers by master map maker Ken Eastin. It was a multistep process that began with the base information from the Ouachita Trail map provided by the Forest Service. We feel that the information on these is pretty accurate— let me know anytime that you find out otherwise. All of the Ranger Districts had an opportunity to view the maps and offer suggestions, and did so again for this revised edition. New re-routes will bring changes to the trail, so be on the look out for them (although you may never even notice them if you are just following along the trail and enjoying yourself!).

There are no contours on the maps—for many folks that just clutters things up. If you feel the need to have a quad map with you, it takes 29 to cover the trail from end-to-end. The maps for a particular section are listed at the front of that section. The trail is not shown on regular USGS quads.

Contour maps that do show the route of the OT are available

in a **three-map waterproof series published by Underwood Geographics and available at outdoor stores and online.** There is lots of detailed OT info including **shelters, mileposts, water sources; plus it shows side trails and many other points of interest along the general trail corridor.** HIGHLY RECOMMENDED companions to this guidebook.

The OT has a *milepost* every mile along it, beginning at Talimena State Park in Oklahoma (#0), and going to Pinnacle Mtn. (#222). The mileposts are small sections of carsonite posts nailed to trees with the mile point on them (see photo on page 1). You may also find some of the original Forest Service mile markers, which were on small aluminum plates attached to low posts that were buried in the ground at ground level. While these tended to get covered up quickly by dead leaves or poison ivy vines, children playing without parental supervision seemed to be able to locate them easily and many of the plates were stolen. The newer mileposts are much easier to see.

The running description of the trail in the text is keyed to these mile points. By using them just like the mile points on an Interstate, it is easy to figure out just exactly where you are, how far you've come, and how far you've got to go. You can also use these mile points to pinpoint problem areas on the trail when you report them to the Forest Service.

The *mileages* shown on the maps and quoted in the text are taken directly from two different logs of the trail that were wheeled off (one by the Forest Service and one by me), and since they both match, I feel pretty good about the figures quoted. All of them have been rounded off to the nearest tenth. I pushed a wheel on my entire hike, and used a tape recorder to note locations by miles and feet. This is the best way that I know of to produce the most accurate information possible. *Future re-routes may alter this of course, but only for that spot.*

There is a mileage chart at the beginning of each section that lists the major trail points, their mile point, and the mileages from both ends of that section. There is also a chart for the entire trail on page 24.

The *elevation profiles* at the bottom of each map were not designed to be an exact replica of all the ups and downs on the trail. There is just simply not enough room to do that in this book. They instead show the relative gain or loss of elevation along the route. And since they are tied to many of the major trail points, you can get a good idea of what lies ahead (a big climb, or an easy downhill). Each section begins at zero on the charts, so that you can figure everything out relative to the distance from the beginning of that section. There is also a mile point number listed below that corresponds to the trail points.

GPS COORDINATES

See page 133 for a coordinates/waypoints list of important trail points—these are shown in *Lat/Lon Digital Degrees — WGS 84* format.

CAMPING

There are five campgrounds along the OT: Talimena State Park, Winding Stair, Queen Wilhelmina State Park, Big Brushy and Lake Sylvia. There is also a campground at the Rich Mtn. Store, a mile west of the Black Fork Mtn. Trailhead on Hwy. 270, and at Iron Springs, which is about a mile and a half south of the trail crossing on Hwy. 7.

Outside of these campgrounds, you are allowed to camp anywhere along the trail in the National Forest (this is true of most National Forests). Camping is restricted along the trail through Queen Wilhelmina State Park, and the last 30 miles on the eastern end.

When you camp in the Forest, you need to be careful and practice low-impact techniques, so as not to damage the area. Please refer to the "Low Impact Use" section here for more details.

REGULATIONS

There are very few rules and regulations that pertain specifically to the OT. If you use common sense, and follow the guidelines under the "Low Impact Use" section that follows, you will be OK. *No permits are needed to camp or hike along the trail.* Most of the campgrounds do charge a fee however. And you do need a permit to park overnight at the Pinnacle Mountain Visitor Center.

Horses and other pack stock are not allowed on the OT. Mountain bikes are allowed on much of the trail—see note below. The Forest Service has been very successful working with various user groups to establish more multi-use trails in the area, and this practice will continue.

The trail is under the same rules and regulations that govern the National Forest or State Park that it happens to be on, and these are usually posted at the trailheads.

MOUNTAIN BIKES

In the early 2000's the forest service opened up 137 miles of the Ouachita Trail for mountain bike use. This new and expanding community has been a great asset to the OT and helps promote and maintain the trail. Hikers and bikers are now sharing the same trail and the same volunteer work and are getting along great. Bikes are not allowed in the wilderness areas or state parks, nor on any of the trail east of Hwy. 7. The OT is open to bike use from the western boundary of the Ouachita National Forest in Oklahoma to the Big Cedar trailhead on Highway 259 (mile 0.0 to 30.5), and from the Talimena Scenic Drive east of Queen Wilhelmena State Park to the trailhead on Highway 7, north of Jessieville (mile 54.1 to 160.7).

WATER

This is a serious subject on the OT. The problem on much of

the trail is that there just simply isn't any. There are stretches of this trail that during real dry months may not have any water on them at all for ten or more miles. Even during the wet season, since a lot of the OT is high up on the ridgetops, you will not find water for miles at a time. I have tried to point out the stretches that are the worst, and note just exactly where the water sources are, and how reliable they are.

The simple fact is that even the largest creeks could dry up in a bad year. And many of them do so every summer. My advice is this: Pay attention to the warnings and suggestions in the text, and don't hike on those dry sections in July, August or September. There are sections that have lots of water, so if you hike in the summer, pick your sections carefully. And carry lots of water!

On the other side of the coin, I hiked the entire trail in March, and only carried one liter of water at a time. I was able to always find plenty to drink, although a couple of times I was down to my last swallow, and was getting a little concerned. I've been told more than once that I resemble a camel. Hum.

I talk a lot about the "wet season" or the "dry season" in the text. It would be easy to say that July-September would be the dry season, March-May the wet season, and all the other months were in between. But it's not quite that easy. I've seen a lot of wet Julys, and a few dry Aprils. Here is one way that I use to get a feel for what to expect on the trail. Look around you as you are heading for the trailhead. Look at the smaller creeks and streams. Are they flowing? Dry? If most of what you see is dry, guess what—carry more water. If they are all flowing well, even the small ones, then you will probably see lots of water along the trail. The bottom line is to always carry more water than you think you will need.

There are red "**W**" symbols on the maps at certain locations. These indicate that you can find water there most, *but not necessarily all*, of the year. It is impossible to tell whether a creek, or for that matter even a spring, will go dry.

Check the FoOT web page for a list of many current water source locations (**friendsoftheouachita.org**).

The water quality in the Ouachita Mountains is excellent, and is generally clean and free of pollution. But that doesn't mean that it won't make you sick. There are lots of tiny critters swimming around in the water that may not match what your system is used to, *even in the springs*. It is best to be sure and treat *all* the water that you drink out on the trail. You can use tablets, iodine crystals, water filters (all available at your local outdoor store), or simply boil your water. For short hikes, I usually carry "Pola Pure" iodine crystals. On longer hikes, I carry a "First Need," "Pur" or other filter. If you don't like the taste of tablets or iodine, then use a filter, or lots of lemonade.

11

PARKING AND ACCESS POINTS

You can pick up the OT at dozens of locations along the way. The best spots are marked on the maps as either a **P** symbol for a "Trailhead Parking" area, or an **A** symbol for an "Access Point" area.

The access points are usually areas where the trail crosses a road, or has a spur trail going up to a small parking area. These are not formal trailheads, usually don't have a lot of room to park, but you may leave your car there.

The Trailhead Parking areas usually have a lot more space to park, have some sort of signboard, and are usually signed from the highway or road. Vehicles are not allowed overnight at Pinnacle Mtn. State Park, except at the Visitor Center lot, and only then after you have checked with their office and received a permit (gates locked at 10pm).

SHUTTLE SERVICE

The OT is a one-way trail, it does not loop. There are several loop trails that connect with it, and in fact use part of it as part of the loop. But if you are hiking just the OT, you will either need to spot a vehicle at the other end, try to hitchhike back to your vehicle when you are done, turn around and hike back the same way that you came, or hire a shuttle service. Here are some commercial folks that do shuttles:

- Ouachita Trail Guide—918–383–0060, *(not related to this guidebook)*
- Woodswitch Farm, Mena, AR—479–437–3549, **www.woodswitch.com**
- Bluebell Cafe & Store, near Mt. Ida and OT mile #122, 870–867–3999
- Ouachita River Haven Resort, near Mt. Ida, AR— 870–326–4941 or 877–314–2836 , **www.ouachitahaven.com**

Check the FoOT web page for other folks who do shuttles and the most current contact info (**friendsoftheouachita.org**).

SHELTERS

The Forest Service and FoOT volunteers have built a system of AT-style shelters along the western and middle sections of the OT from mile 9.4 to mile 189.5. These are three-sided log shelters with a wood floor, and have room to sleep a number of folks and store gear out of the weather. Each shelter has a picnic table, fire grate, broom, and logbook. While they are *sometimes* located near a water source, that source may be dry in the summer, so be sure to plan ahead and *always* carry water. They sure are a welcome sight when it's pouring rain!

The first nine shelters were built by the forest service and are located in the middle sections of the OT. A dozen new shelters were built by FoOT volunteers in the western sections of the OT and are listed in the mileages (pages 24–25) and GPS logs (pages 133–135) in this guidebook. The final three of these shelters were completed in 2016, making a total of 21 shelters along the OT. YIPPIE! Volunteers continue to rehab and upgrade the shelters as needed, but can always use more help! See the FoOT website for the latest details more info at **www.friendsoftheouachita.org.**

LOW IMPACT USE

As the OT gets more and more use, we need to be especially careful that we don't impact the special areas along it. It's easy to destroy a fragile spot, but it's just as easy to tread lightly and keep from messing up the things that we came out to see in the first place. All it takes is a little common sense. If we all do our part, this wonderful trail of ours will stay that way so that generations to follow will be able to enjoy the raw scenic beauty that we do.

Stay on the trail. The OT was designed to carry you from one point to another in the most efficient (and/or scenic) way. When folks cut switchbacks, erosion begins, and soon the trail is messed up and there is an ugly scar. It is not rude to ask someone that you see doing this to kindly get back on the trail.

Hike in small groups. It's fun to go out with a large gang, but that doesn't always work too well in the backcountry—it destroys the character and solitude of the place. Not to mention increasing the possibility of damage to the trail and surrounding areas. Always limit the size of your group to 10 or less when you're going to be camping. Fewer is generally better. Besides, you'll have more campsite selection if you only have one or two tents to set up. Have your parties at home—come to the woods to enjoy nature, not Billboard's Top-10. Speaking of noise, be considerate of others—they just might be out on the trail to get away from all the hustle and bustle of city life—enjoy the peaceful solitude, and let others do the same.

Camp in established sites when possible. Overnight stays have more impact on the land than probably anything else we do while hiking. If everyone camped in a new location every night, the damage would be much more widespread. By concentrating this damage to several sites, the area will stay more primitive. If you must set up in a new spot, choose a site *at least 100 feet away from the trail* and any water source, and preferably out of sight (*and please, please don't build a new fire ring*). I hate to hike down a nice trail and see tents scattered along the way. Don't you? I realize that many of the good campsites along the OT are closer to the trail and/or water than 100 feet, but try to get further away if you can.

Protect our water. Clean water adds so much to the outdoor experience, not to mention our quality of life in general. Here is a simple guideline to remember when in the backcountry—don't put *anything* into the water. Period! I know, I know, you use "biodegradable soap." What if the guy just upstream is using it too, and takes a bath in the creek that you're getting your kool aid water out of? You'll have suds in your punch! Oh yea, it will be biodegradable punch, but suds just the same. Yuk! Think about downstream—we all live there. Use biodegradable soap if you have to, but use it *away* from the stream. Or better yet, don't use soap of any kind.

Keep bathroom duties out of sight. This is rather obvious, but not everyone seems to understand. You need to get completely out of sight of the trail and any water supply to do your business. Dig a small hole, fill it in and cover it up when you're done. Why do people still leave their mess next to the trail?

Cook with a stove. We haven't reached a firewood shortage yet along the OT, but if we all built big fires every day, we would have one. Do all of your cooking with one of the lightweight stoves available. They're quicker and a whole lot cleaner anyway. Campfires are OK, but keep them small, *don't* build a fire ring, and only use dead branches that are on the ground and that you can break with your hands—if you have to saw it, it's too darn big! (Large wood seldom ever burns up completely, and what you have left over is an ugly black stick.)

Leave No Trace. This should be your goal on any trip on a trail, no matter where it is—when you leave there should be no sign of your ever having been there. It really seems silly to even mention this, but because there are still a few stupid people in the woods, I will—**Pack It In, Pack It Out**—don't litter! Don't carve up trees. Don't cut or destroy *any* living thing. Leave it as you found it. In fact, leave it cleaner than you found it—carry a trash bag for not only your own stuff, but for other litter that you see along the way too.

WILDERNESS AREAS

The OT goes through the middle of two Federally designated Wilderness Areas, the Upper Kiamichi River Wilderness in Oklahoma, and the Flatside Wilderness in Arkansas. Mechanized vehicles (including mountain bikes) and motors of any type are not allowed in these areas. The areas are managed keep them in a pristine condition, which means there is very little management inside at all (except, of course, for the *people* in them, which do take a lot of managing). There is, however, a great deal that is done on the outside to try to protect these special areas. *The biggest threat to wilderness areas is man.*

HIKING PACE

The question that I get asked most often is "how far can I hike in a day?" That is a good question, and no one knows the answer to that except *you*. How far or how fast you hike is determined by many different factors, the least of which is the trail. Much of the OT is built to standards which enable average folks to hike it with no problem. If the hill gets a little too steep (which it *does* do on the OT a number of times), just slow down, and enjoy the view.

Generally speaking, if you are an average hiker, including rest stops and lunch, you can probably average about a mile an hour when you are carrying a backpack. Most people who don't **backpack** much, *and there is a big difference between backpacking and just hiking with no weight on your back*, can hike six to ten miles a day without too much trouble. Although it's been my experience that for most people less miles and more time to look around is best.

If you are in good shape, hike a lot, and aren't interested in spending a great deal of time messing around, sure you can hike fifteen or more miles a day. When I go out and get serious, I average about three miles an hour, and typically cover twenty plus miles a day. But, of course, it hurts.

I hiked the OT end-to-end in 12 days when doing the log for this guidebook. I often left my tent at first light, and usually hiked until nearly dark. I also carried a very lightweight pack. I basically never stopped to smell the flowers, I kept going. I would say that the trail can be hiked in two weeks or less, but I would probably recommend that you take three or more weeks to do it.

SPEED RECORDS. The fastest hike reported to me of the entire trail to date was done by Greg Eason and Steve Kirk who did the trail in 76 hours, 33 minutes, and one second in December, 2005. Also Fawn Hernandez is listed on the "Fastest Known Time" web page of 3 days, 22 hours, and 14 minutes ending on April 1, 2021.

A WORD OF CAUTION. When it is cold out you tend to start hiking with too many clothes on, and soon break out in a sweat. *This can kill you*, and you may not even realize what is happening. Of course, I'm talking about hypothermia. I'm not going to tell you all about it or how to treat it—you should read up on it though before you go into the woods. But I will say this—use the "layering method" when you hike, i.e. remove clothing as you get warm, and always hike so that you don't work up a sweat (slow down your pace if you have to). In fact, I always start off feeling slightly chilled in colder weather, knowing that my motor (and the hill ahead) will heat things up soon enough.

FIRES

Open fires are allowed on most of the OT, and permits are not required. But, as just discussed, limit your use of campfires. Here are a few points to remember. *New fire rings are not allowed.* If you aren't camping in an area that already has a fire ring, then please don't build one. It isn't really necessary (cook on your stove), and the blackened rocks will be an ugly scar for a long time.

To build a low-impact fire, first clear away all of the leaves and other duff, down to bear dirt. Build a small fire in the middle of the cleared-out area. Use dead branches that are on the ground, not broken from tree trunks. I usually build a "pile fire"—add alternate layers of leaves and small twigs. As the leaves burn, the twigs will too. Gradually add bigger twigs until they will burn each other. It's not too pretty, and does get a little smoky, but it's the fastest and easiest way that I know to build a small fire.

When you are finished, and this is the most important step of all, make sure that your fire is *completely out*. Drown it, stir it, drown it, and stir it again. You've all seen those Smoky The Bear commercials. He isn't kidding. It's a shame to burn down a wonderful forest. And guess what, if you accidently start a forest fire, *you* may get a bill for what it cost to put it out. You should be able to lay your hand on the fire and not feel **any** heat. Once you're convinced that it's dead out, cover the area with leaves and twigs so that you can't tell you've built a fire there.

WILDLIFE, INCLUDING SNAKES AND BEARS

There is an abundance of wildlife along the OT, both large and small. I have seen everything from colorful lizards and hummingbirds, to bald eagles, deer, turkeys and bears. Most of these critters will flee at the first sign (or noise) of a hiker, so you probably won't see many while you are hiking. But when you stop and take time out, that is another story. On my last hike of the OT in March, I actually saw over 300 turkeys while I was hiking. *Three hundred!*

Yes, there are bears. Black bears have been stocked by the Arkansas Game and Fish Commission for many years (lots have wandered over into Oklahoma). They are not the huge grizzlies that you hear and see so much of on TV though. They are pretty small, actually about the same size as you and me. And, they aren't really much of a problem. We have only had one incident of physical harm to a hiker that I'm aware of. I have been hiking for 34 years, and I have only seen four bears in all that time (in Ark/Okla area). Most of them will take off just as fast as they can, if they see or scent you. Any loud noise will usually send a curious one off into the woods in a hurry. If you see a bear, and it is obvious that he has seen you, shout at the top of your lungs. If that doesn't work, good luck.

Even though bears have not been much of a problem in the past, that doesn't mean that you can ignore them. They are strong, and under the wrong circumstances, can be quite dangerous. Although it's probably not a necessity to "bear bag" your food when you camp, it's a good idea. *Do not keep food in your tent with you* though. I use a bear-proof container now to keep my food in, and to stash at midway trailheads. They work great, and are no trouble.

There have been increasing reports of bears in the areas near the first three sections of the OT. So your chances of seeing one are generally much greater on that end of the trail.

And yes, there are snakes. Lots of snakes. Copperheads. Rattlesnakes. And cottonmouths. And they do bite. But snake bites are rare, and are usually the result of someone playing with one. Bees kill more people nationwide than snakes do, so it's not a real serious problem. But they are there. Watch out for them. Look at them. But for goodness sakes, don't play with them. A snake will not seek you out and bite you. If you reach down and pick one up, or happen to step on one, sure it will bite you. What else can it do? Watch your step, mind your own business, and you shouldn't have any problems.

If you do happen to get bit, the best thing that you can do is relax, you aren't going to die. And get to a doctor as soon as you can. Most people don't know how to use a snakebite kit, so they aren't much good. I do recommend that you carry a device called "The Extractor"—it does work (on bee stings too). The main thing is to just try and stay out of their way.

I'm not much of a bird person, but I can tell you that there are lots and lots of birds out there. A good exercise is to take a bird book with you and try to identify a different species every day of your hike.

HUNTING AND FISHING

Arkansas and Oklahoma have an abundance of game animals. The large numbers of hunters and fisherman are responsible for a lot of the wildlife being here in such large numbers. You see, their hunting and fishing licenses support the aggressive stocking programs of both game and nongame species throughout each state. Licenses are required of all resident and nonresident sportsman over the age of 16. Check with the Arkansas Game and Fish Commission and Oklahoma Department of Wildlife Conservation for more information (their addresses are on page 134).

There are few conflicts between hunters and hikers. A lot of folks are afraid to hike during the hunting season. There is a hunting season of one sort or another going on from September through the middle of June. Why would you want to stay home during all of the best hiking seasons? Most of the trail is open to hunting, and you will see hunters, especially in November (deer season) and April (turkey season). Be polite and get along. They belong on the trail too. It is always a good idea to wear a blaze orange vest over your pack then.

There aren't any opportunities for fishing along the OT for the first 195 miles or so, until you get to the Maumelle River. Fishing is excellent from there on, in the river, and Lake Maumelle. I take that back, I've heard that Lake Sylvia is pretty good too.

BUGS

There are all kinds of bugs out there along the OT. Mosquitoes start to come out near the end of April and May. Ticks too. And chiggers like to show up during the summer. And just about the time that they are all getting burned up by the dry weather and heat, horseflies and gnats come out and really bug you.

There is no surefire way to keep them all from bothering you. A good 100% DEET repellent will help. *Greenban* is good too, and doesn't contain the harsh DEET chemical. Neither does Avon *Skin-So-Soft*, which works great for some people, not at all for others.

In addition to repellents, a couple of other things will help too. First, don't smell good. Take a shower before you go into the woods, but don't *add* any sweet scents to your body. And campfire smoke really knocks down the bugs. It smells a lot better than perfume anyway. In fact, you might say that campfire smoke is trail perfume.

In July, August and September, the spider webs across the trail just drive you nuts. A headnet will usually do the trick, but then you don't get as much protein that way—the net will keep you from accidentally eating those fat rascals! This is a good time of the year to hike with a tall friend—let them lead.

By late October most of the bugs should be gone until spring. Although I have seen ticks out all winter before. And speaking of ticks, they have been getting a lot of press lately, and I think that many folks are just plain afraid to go into the woods anymore. If you find a tick on you, just reach down and pull it off. No big deal. However, since Lyme disease is becoming more prevalent, if you suspect a problem, not only go to a doctor, but *tell* him that you've been in the woods and to consider ticks as a culprit (it's easily treatable if caught in time).

SEASONS

Spring. An excellent time to hike. It's very magical along the OT in March and April as everything comes to life. There's usually a lot more water too. Of course, we've got lots of wildflowers, but the trees flower wildly as well. Especially the dogwoods, redbuds, serviceberry, and wild plums. Some of the ridges were so fragrant from the plum blooms that I had trouble breathing (or was it the climb up?).

Summer. It gets pretty hot and muggy towards June, July and August. Everyone heads to the lakes. The trail is very dry, and water becomes a *major* problem. I would strongly recommend that you not hike the OT in July, August and September. If you do, stick to the areas that have a large stream, and spend your time sitting in it. If you are able to carry enough water, you will probably have the trail to yourself and get in some pretty good hiking. One of my favorite things is getting caught out in a summer thunderstorm.

Fall. Each season has a certain smell to it, but none so nice as the scent of a crisp October or November day in the woods. Forget about all the blaze of color. Forget the deep blue sky. Forget the craft fairs. Fall just *feels* so good! Pick any part of the trail, and you'll have a great hike. If you are looking for spectacular colors, and there will be lots, try the west end of the trail in early to mid November (call Queen Wilhelmina State Park for current conditions). Fall is also the prime hunting season, and most of the OT is open to hunting. You shouldn't be afraid to hike then, but do be aware of what is going on.

Winter. This is the longest hiking season on the OT. Some years we have long stretches of 60–70 degree days, with brilliant sunshine. Much of the trail that runs through an endless tunnel of heavy forest the rest of the year, is now open to the world—with no leaves on the trees you can see deep into the hills and hollows, and out across the countryside. There are no bugs or snakes, and seldom other hikers. Of course, it can get down right nasty too. Especially up at high altitude on Winding Stair or Rich Mountain—they get some pretty bad weather in the winter. The bottom line here is *be prepared.*

WEATHER

The weather is difficult to predict and constantly changing. Here is a breakdown by month of the type of weather that you are likely to see while hiking. There are certainly no absolutes, because it is just as likely to be 70 degrees on Christmas Day as it is to be 0. But here are some averages.

January. This is a great month to hike. Lots of nice, clear views, and probably some ice formations too. It is one of the coldest months. Daytime highs in the 30's and 40's, with some days in the 50's and even 60's. Nighttime lows may be in the teens and twenties, but often down to 0, and once in a while below for a short period. It may snow some, but not too much, and probably won't stay around for long. Rain is likely too. But the real killer is an ice storm. They don't happen too often. When they do, the forest is just incredible.

February. Expect weather just like January. Possibly a little colder. Witch hazel bushes will pop open on sunny afternoons along the streams (especially Big Cedar, Kiamichi and Irons Fork), and the fragrance will soothe the beast in you. I wish that they made a perfume that smelled like this.

March. Things are beginning to warm up, and get a little wetter. Daytime highs in the 50's and 60's, sometimes up into the 70's. Nighttime lows are milder, in the 30's and 40's, with a cold snap down into the 20's once in a while. Some snow, but not much. There are often long, soaking rains. Wildflowers begin to pop out. Serviceberry, redbud and wild plum trees come out and show their colors too.

April. One of the best months of the year. Daytime temps reach into the 70's and even some 80's. The mild nights are in the 40's and 50's, with still a cold snap once in a great while. Sometimes a heavy, wet snow, but this is rare. There can be some great spring thunderstorms. It's a wet month, and the few waterfalls along the trail usually are running at full tilt. Wildflowers are everywhere. And the dogwoods pop out in full bloom, and they are the most common understory tree so it is quite a sight. The rest of the trees begin to green up too. And, as a photographer I notice this, the new growth is just a brilliant kind of green that you don't see at any other time of the year. Be on the lookout for turkey hunters.

May. Another great month, and it is the wettest month of the year. It may rain for days on end. The daytime temps reach into the upper 80's, and the nights seldom get below 60. Wild azaleas are in full bloom now. And there are still lots of wildflowers around. And plenty of sunshine. The trees are all leafed out now.

June. Still good hiking weather. Less rain, and warmer. Days may reach 90, and it will drop into the 70's at night. This is the last really good month to hike for a while. The bugs start to come out, and the humidity goes up a little. Also the trail gets grown up with weeds, briars and other unmentionables. Time for long pants!

July. This is an "ify" month. It could be cool and wet, but most of the time it is pretty dry and beginning to get hot, up into the 90's, with nights still down into the 70's, or even 60's. When it does rain, it usually does so with lots of power. It's a wonderful experience to hike in the warm rain though. Try it sometime.

August. This is a good month to go to the beach or lake. Not a good time to be out hiking the OT. In fact, I recommend once again that you not hike the trail then, unless you just have to. And only then if you are able to carry all of the water that you need, because you probably won't find too much along the trail. Especially along the western half of the trail. The eastern half is a little more forgiving. This would be a good time to hike the eastern end around Lake Maumelle. Daytime highs can reach 100, with humidity readings to match. Sometimes it doesn't get below 80 at night. And there are lots of ticks, chiggers and other assorted bugs just waiting for you. And lots of spider webs strung across the trail. So if you do go hiking, go with someone else and let them lead (or wear a headnet).

September. This is also a good month to stay home. It is often a worse month than August. Everything is pretty much the same except that horseflies come out, and they are really a pain. Towards the end of the month, it does begin to cool off a bit. That's a good sign that better hiking is just around the corner, so you had better dust off that equipment, and maybe get into shape. Try doing some early morning hikes. You'll be surprised at who else you'll find out there on the trails with you.

October. This is the other best month of the year. The first part of it is usually still quite warm, dry and buggy. But towards the middle the nights get cooler, down into the 50's, 40's and even 30's, and then it frosts. Yet the days are in the 70's and some 80's. By the end of the month it's crisp, clear days and nights. The bugs are pretty much gone too. Great hiking weather.

November. Early in the month is still kind of like October, only something happens—the hardwood forests transform from the dull green that you have gotten used to since May, into one of the most incredible displays of color anywhere. It can be just as pretty as New England or Colorado. There are still some warm days, but it can change quickly. Towards the end of the month, the leaves die and fall off of the trees. This turns everything the same color of brown, but also opens up lots of views that have been hidden since April. Of course, the pine forests pretty much stay the same color, which is a welcome sight in the winter. The days get cooler, down into the 40's and even 30's, with some nice warm days in the 60's. The nights fall into the 20's and 30's more often, and once in a while there will be a cold snap. Rain is more frequent, and once in a great while, some snow. This is the month when hunters are most active, especially in the Oklahoma sections.

December. A good month to hike. The days are usually in the 30's and 40's, but are often in the 50's and above. The nights get cold, and can drop down to zero once in a while. Snow is more likely, but not too much. And it can rain a lot. This is a typical flood month, though it is usually pretty dry, with some rain now and then, and once in a while some ice. A campfire feels great.

GLOSSARY OF TERMS

Here are a few words that I use over and over again in this guide that you may not be familiar with.

Bench. This is part of a hill, a section that is usually level and runs along the hill for a while. If there was a giant around he could sit on it, like a bench.

Climb, ease, head. I use all of these, and probably a couple more to describe the relative steepness of the trail. And you can pretty much relate them to your breathing. When the trail "eases" up the hill, it does so just barely, and your breathing won't change. When it "heads" up the hill, it takes a little more effort to go, and you will begin to breathe a little harder (depending on how heavy your pack is). If the trail "climbs" up the hill, then plan on doing some heaving breathing, especially if I say that it "climbs steeply." You should hear my recorded tape of this hike—on some of the climbs in Oklahoma you can hardly understand what I'm trying to say because I'm huffing and puffing.

Drain (creek, stream, river). A drain is a small stream drainage, often rocky, that seldom has any water in it. When it rains hard, it will usually run some. I say "dry drain" a lot because most of them are. Drains can be interesting spots. *Creeks* and *streams* are larger and will have water flowing in them. A *river* is the largest of all, and flows all year. And a *seep* is just a wet spot, usually from a tiny, often unseen spring.

FR#. This is the name of a forest road, and will be followed by a number, like FR #1003. These are roads built and maintained by the

U.S. Forest Service, and are usually dirt or gravel.

Leaf-off. This is the season after all the leaves on the trees fall off, and before they grow new ones in the spring. There are always a lot more views out through the trees during leaf-off.

Quad. A standard 7 1/2 minute USGS quadrangle map with 20 foot contours . Very detailed, but not a necessity to hike the OT.

Reindeer. Well, you probably know what real reindeer are, but we have tons of the other kind along the OT. These are actually *reindeer lichens*, which are thick, grey-colored, neat-looking structures that grow as ground cover and often on rocks. I don't remember if they get their name because reindeer eat them, or because the actual organism looks like a tangled pile of reindeer horns. Most of the time they are quite soft and spongy, but in the winter they get brittle and fragile. It is best to observe, enjoy and *leave* in place. I will usually refer to a clump of them as simply "reindeer" (this drove my editor nuts).

Road trace. These are old roads that have not been used for a while, and are usually grown up with trees and other vegetation, and/ or covered over with deep duff. They often make great trails because they are wide enough to allow two hikers to walk side-by-side and carry on a conversation. Jeep roads and four-wheeler trails are basically old road traces that are being used by these vehicles.

Saddle. This is a low spot in a ridge. Trails like to pass through them because it's easier than climbing all the way to the top. You will read this word over and over and over and over in this guidebook. Saddles are pretty neat places though, and make great campsites.

SSS. This means **"Special Scenic Spot."** There are a lot of places along the trail that may or may not be well known, but are just neat little areas that I find very attractive. The better sections of the OT have more SSS's!

Wizard Tree. These are oak trees that are stunted and gnarled and kind of remind me of those apple trees in the Wizard of Oz. I often simply refer to them as "wizards."

Up-and-downing. This term is used a lot, and is pretty much self explanatory. This is where the trail goes up the hillside some (not too steep), then soon goes down the hillside some (again, not too steep).

LOST IN THE WOODS

I have always hiked alone most of the time, and have more or less decided that if anything serious ever happened to me, well, then I would either make it home or I would end my life in one of the most beautiful places in the world. When there are other people involved, then you have to start thinking about what to do and how to get help if something goes wrong.

It's a good idea to have this guide with you when you are on the trail. If you do have a problem and have to get to help in a hurry, you will be able to tell where you are and find a road that will get you to help. And you should always sign in at every trail register.

If you get lost, there are two things that you can do. If you feel pretty confident in your ability, then you should just try and figure it out, and then make an attempt to get un-lost. Sometimes this may involve following a stream a couple of miles to a forest road, and then walking a few more miles around to a known spot or help.

If you are really lost and have no hope of finding your way, then lets hope that there are other hikers, hunters or someone else in that particular section of woods. The best thing to do is get comfortable, make yourself at home, and start a fire. Eventually someone will come looking for you. The main thing is to not panic. Panic kills. So you end up spending a day or two in the woods that you hadn't counted on. It just might be the best thing that has happened to you in a while. Remember, stay calm. You'll be all right. And stay put.

THANK YOU'S

There were quite a few folks—including hikers as well as forest service personnel—who helped me keep track of changes in the OT over the years, and I have tried to include all of their suggestions in this revised copy of the book. In particular many members of the Friends of the Ouachita Trail (FoOT) have been my eyes and feet as they have covered every inch of the trail this past year or two. While the list of helpful folks is long, two in particular have been the most help. Kris McMillen and Jim Gifford formed the new volunteer FoOT organization that has saved the OT, and both have given me bucketloads of important data. And Kris went a step or two farther, hiking the entire OT in 2004, keeping careful notes along the way. When Kris casually sent me a brief e-mail right after her trip with a couple of suggestions, she had no idea that I would badger her for months and months, finally getting tons of corrections and updates from her. She has quickly become the "Jim Rawlins" of the new century. We are all fortunate to have Kris, Jim, and all the volunteers of FoOT out there working on our side—way to go guys, and keep up the terrific work!

By the way, is has been more than 30 years since I first shared a trail with the great Jim Rawlins, the grandpappy of the OT. He remains in good health and is the same sly character he has always been. We both wish all of you many wonderful, safe, and enjoyable miles on the OT.

See ya in the woods...

Tim Ernst

MILEAGE LOG

Trail Point	Mile Point and Mileage West to East	Mileage East to West
Talimena State Park	0.0	222.5
Military Road Trail	.7	221.8
Potato Hills Vista Spur	2.4	220.1
Panorama Vista Spur	5.0	217.5
FR #6010	5.8	216.7
Deadman's Gap	8.0	214.5
Boardstand Trail	8.7	213.8
Rock Garden Shelter	9.4	213.1
Cedar Branch Branch	11.2	211.3
Wildhorse Creek	13.9	208.6
Holson Valley Vista Shelter	16.8	205.7
Horsethief Trail	18.7	203.8
Horsethief Springs	19.9	202.6
FR #6014	21.7	200.8
Billy Creek Trail	22.4	200.1
Winding Stair	23.7	198.8
Winding Stairs Shelter/Tower	25.0	197.5
Rough Mountain	27.0	195.5
Red Spring	28.4	194.1
Big Cedar Creek	30.3	192.2
Hwy. 259	30.5	192.0
Pashubbe Shelter	34.0	188.5
Pashubbe Trailhead	34.3	188.2
Wilton Mountain	36.7	185.8
Kiamichi River, #1	40.9	181.6
Kiamichi River, #8	45.0	177.5
Arkansas State Line	46.3	176.2
State Line Shelter	46.4	176.1
Pioneer Cemetery	49.5	173.0
Queen Wilhelmina S.P.	51.6	170.9
Talimena Scenic Drive	54.1	168.2
Hwy. 270 Trailhead	56.7	165.6
Black Fork Mountain Trail	57.8	164.7
Black Fork Mountain Shelter	57.8 (+.1)	164.7 (+.1)
Eagle Gap/Clear Fork	58.5	164.0
Foran Gap/Hwy. 71	68.1	154.4
Foran Gap Shelter	68.9	153.6
Tan-a-Hill Gap	74.1	148.4
Tan-a-Hill Spring	74.2 (+.3)	148.3 (+.3)
Turner Gap Shelter	79.9	142.6
FR #76	86.0	136.5
FR #48	88.2	134.3
FR #813	90.3	132.2
Brushy Creek Mtn. Shelter	90.6	131.9
Brushy Creek Trail	91.4	131.1
Big Brushy Campground	94.5	128.0
FR #33	96.0	126.5
Blowout Mountain	96.8	125.7
Fiddler Creek Shelter	100.9	121.6
Fiddlers Creek/FR #274	101.1	121.4
FR #149	105.5	117.0
Rainy Creek	105.6	116.9
Suck Mountain Shelter	108.6	113.9
Suck Mountain	108.7	113.8

Trail Point	Mile Point and Mileage West to East	Mileage East to West
Round Top Trail	114.1	108.4
Story Cr. Shelter/spring	116.7	105.8
Womble Trail	117.2	105.3
FR #149/Muddy Creek	118.7	103.8
Smith Creek	121.1	101.4
Hwy. 27	121.7	100.8
John Archer Shelter Spur	122.6	99.9
FR #148	124.2	98.3
Uncle Potter Shelter Spur	127.5	95.0
Irons Fork Creek	128.8	93.7
FR #78 North cross	133.6	88.9
Big Branch Shelter Spur	134.0	88.5
FR #78 South cross	136.1	86.4
County Rd. 139/Taber Mtn.Rd	136.9	85.6
Hwy. 298 Trailhead	138.8	83.7
Blue Mountain Shelter Spur	143.2	79.3
Ouachita Pinnacle	147.0	75.5
FR #107	147.8	74.7
Blocker Creek	148.0	74.5
Big Bear Shelter Spur	150.7	71.7
Old FR #107 (closed)	153.0	69.5
Hoot Owl Gap	155.1	67.4
FR #122/Blakely Creek	157.0	65.5
Moonshine Shelter Spur	158.4	64.1
Hunts Loop Trail	159.4	63.1
Hwy. 7 Trailhead	160.4	62.1
FR #132	162.3	60.2
Sugar Creek	163.9	58.6
FR #153	165.4	57.1
Oak Mountain Shelter Spur	167.4	55.1
FR #124	168.8	53.7
Green Thumb Spring	170.6	51.9
Grindstone Gap Spur	173.5	49.0
Crystal Prong Creek	177.2	45.3
Flatside Pinnacle Spur	179.4	43.1
FR #805	179.8	42.7
Brown Creek Shelter Spur	182.5	40.0
Brown Creek	183.1	39.4
North Fork Pinnacle Spur	184.8	37.7
Lake Sylvia (via spur)	187.3 (+ .4)	35.2 (+.4)
FR #152	187.4	35.1
Chinquapin Gap	188.7	33.8
Nancy Mountain Shelter	189.5	33.0
Hilary Hollow	190.0	32.5
Hwy. 9 Trailhead	191.8	30.7
National Forest Boundary	192.5	30.0
Maumelle River	195.6	26.9
Red Bluff Creek	196.3	26.2
Hwy. 10, 1st cross	202.0	20.5
Hwy. 113, 2nd cross	204.1	18.4
Sawdust Pile	206.5	16.0
Reece's Creek	208.2	14.3
Penney Campsite Spur	208.4	14.1
Lunsford Corner	212.2	10.3
Lake Maumelle Spillway	219.2	3.3
Pinnacle Mountain Office	222.5	0.0

SECTION ONE—23.7 miles
Talimena State Park to Winding Stair Campground

Trail Point	Mile Point	Mileage West to East	Mileage East to West
State Park	0.0	0.0	23.7
Military Road Trail	.7	.7	23.0
Potato Hills Vista Spur	2.4	2.4	21.3
Panorama Vista Spur	5.0	5.0	18.7
FR #6010	5.8	5.8	17.9
Deadman's Gap (Talimena Scenic Drive)	8.0	8.0	15.7
Boardstand Trail	8.7	8.7	15.0
Rock Garden Shelter	9.4	9.4	14.3
Cedar Branch Branch	11.2	11.2	12.5
Wildhorse Creek	13.9	13.9	9.8
Holson Valley Vista Shelter	16.8	16.8	6.9
Horsethief Trail	18.7	18.7	5.0
Horsethief Springs	19.9	19.9	3.8
FR #6014	21.7	21.7	2.0
Billy Creek Trail	22.4	22.4	1.3
Mountain Top Trail	22.9	22.9	.8
Winding Stair	23.7	23.7	0.0

Section One of the Ouachita Trail (OT) begins at Talimena State Park. All the rest of this section is located in the Ouachita National Forest. It runs across the Kiamichi and Choctaw Ranger Districts of the U.S. Forest Service, but all of the trails on both Districts are managed by the Choctaw District. Their office is in Heavener, Oklahoma (Kiamichi office is in Talihina, OK). Quad maps are Blackjack Ridge, LeFlore SE, Muse (across one corner) and Big Cedar, all in Oklahoma.

All of this section is located within the Winding Stair National Recreation Area (WSNRA), which is a large area of big mountains, steep hills, lush vegetation, and lots of rocks. This is *big* country. Running down the middle of it all, of course, is the Talimena Scenic Drive, a National Scenic Byway (Hwy. 88 in Arkansas and Hwy. 1 in Oklahoma). It runs 53 miles along the crest of Rich and Winding Stair mountains from Mena, Arkansas to near the beginning of the OT in Oklahoma. It is a breathtaking drive to say the least. The trail crosses it a total of three times, once on this section. The OT is breathtaking too, but often for a different reason.

The OT climbs up and runs along Winding Stair Mountain, crosses the Scenic Drive, drops down some on the north side of the mountain, then climbs back up it and runs along it past Horsethief Springs Picnic Area to the Winding Stair Trailhead, which is next to the campground there. This is the most difficult section of the OT to hike.

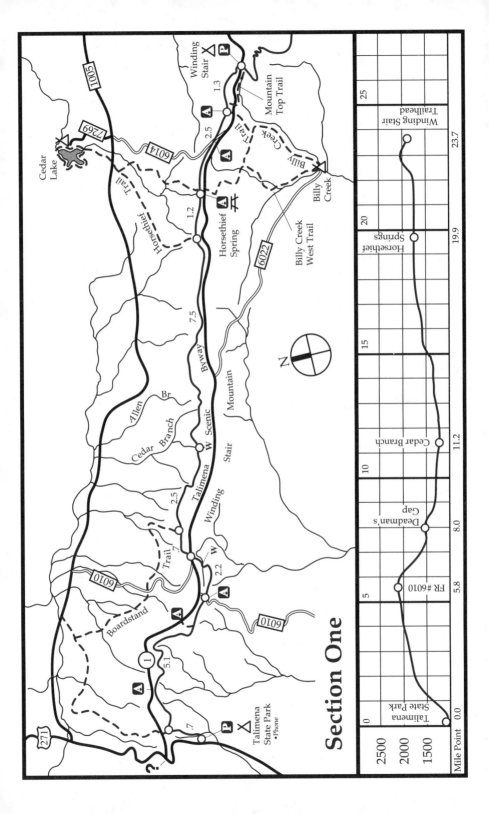

Section One

On the north side of Winding Stair Mountain the trail is nonexistent in many places where it goes through one boulder field after another. And at times it literally climbs straight up the side of the hill. It is all very scenic though, so if you are tough and go slow, you will have a great hike.

Like much of the trail, there is very little water on this section during dry seasons. In fact, **you may only find water two or three times—in the summer you may not find any water at all!** So be sure and carry lots with you. If necessary, you can stash water at Deadman's Gap on the Scenic Drive. During the wet season you will usually find plenty of water though. (You will come to learn that it is not a real good idea to hike this trail in late summer/early fall when many of the streams dry up.)

Talimena State Park is located on Hwy. 271 about a mile south of the western end of the Scenic Drive (there is a Forest Service Visitor Center at the junction of Hwys. 1 and 271). As you turn into the Park, take the middle road, and the trailhead is just on the left. There is an outdoor phone here, so if you hike the trail in the opposite direction than is described here, you can call for help when you arrive.

The trail quickly leaves the campground, heads through a barbed-wire fence (and enters National Forest), through a pine forest. It's mostly level, then eases around to the left and heads downhill slightly. It follows an old road trace for a short distance, past some lichen-covered rocks, then drops down and crosses a creek on plain trail at .4.

From there the trail heads back uphill some, passing several larger pines scattered around the hardwoods. It crosses over a small bridge, and continues *up* the hill at a pretty good clip, swinging back and forth. At .7 there is an intersection—this is the Old Military Road Trail, which goes straight ahead and is blazed WHITE. [If you wanted to make a loop hike in this area, this is the trail to take (or come back on). It connects with the Boardstand Trail, which in turn intersects back with the OT at 8.7. The total loop distance would be 20–25 miles. The Forest Service has a free map of it available.] TURN RIGHT at this intersection and continue to follow the BLUE BLAZES.

It goes up some, then down, then back up, passing an SSS at .8—a boulder-strewn creekbed just down on the right. We drop down and cross that creek on a small bridge soon after. Then it's back uphill again, swinging right and left up the hillside. This is a *steep* climb at times, and continues past mile #1, where there is a "1" painted on the tree. The trail joins an old road trace and remains steep, very steep. This would be a tough climb with a heavy pack (aren't they always). At 1.1, as the road heads off to the right, the trail leaves it TO THE LEFT, continuing uphill steeply.

It does level off somewhat along a ridge, then heads around the right side, mostly level. There are a few views through the pines of the distant ridges. It picks up a road trace briefly, then leaves it up and to the left, and levels off again. The trail is pretty rocky through this area, and the hillside that it is crossing is steep, but the trail remains mostly level. It passes through a couple of small, rocky drains, past some huckleberry bushes, to mile #2, which is also painted on a tree.

You begin to pick up a fence line to the left through here (orange metal posts)—you will see this off and on until the end of this section. This is the highway department boundary for the Scenic Drive. I guess they want to keep hikers from walking on it. Just kidding. Anyway, the trail remains mostly level and rocky. The views are spotty. It does go through an area of scrub oaks that open things up some.

At 2.2 there is a nice lichen-covered boulder field, a minor SSS. Then the trail crosses a small drain on a rock bridge, then cuts a switchback *up* the hill to the left. There are some nice larger boulders along the way up, then it swings back to the right and comes to a trail intersection at 2.4. This spur trail heads up to the left to the Potato Hills Vista on the Scenic Drive—it's not really worth the effort. It is obvious that we are pretty close to the top of the ridge. All of this, by the way, is Winding Stair Mountain, which we will be on one side of or the other for this entire section.

The OT continues STRAIGHT AHEAD at this intersection, on the level. It remains rocky, passing several small drains, dipping downhill once or twice. At 2.8 there is a small glade area, an SSS, as the trail turns to the right and begins downhill some. There are lots of stunted pine trees in this area, and a few larger slab rocks, plus a pretty good view during leaf-off. The trail quickly levels off, and passes through a series of open glade areas as it crosses the steep hillside. Just before mile 3.0, there is a large open area which is our best SSS view yet. A little ways beyond is MILEPOST #3, and the first Forest Service MILEPOST that we've seen.

Each mile from this point on is supposed to have one of these surveyor-type posts, which are aluminum caps attached to a piece of steel rod that is stuck into the ground. The posts are fairly noticeable, but unfortunately many of them have been swiped by thoughtless people. The mile number is stamped in the middle. Some of the trees are painted with the mile number too.

Also at the mile points there are blue painted "OT" symbols. You should find these on a tree on either side of where the mile posts are. You will also find these same painted symbols at road crossings and other areas to signify that the OT goes that direction. And throughout most of the Oklahoma part of the OT, these symbols are also painted on trees at mid-mile spots too, although I wouldn't rely on this too much. For most of the mileposts there will also be a white blaze painted on the tree.

The trail continues on the level, passing more open glade areas, through scrub trees. It does some up-and-downing, past a number of stunted, fat pine trees, and down across a small drain. Then it heads on the level, across a steep hillside with thick underbrush, past a large pine or two, and sporadic views. It crosses another small drain, up a little, past some small bluffs at 3.9. There are more neat, large pines that remind me of small sequoias, then MILEPOST #4. Some of the pines are rather twisted as well—an SSS area of sorts. The hillside is very steep and rocky, but the trail is mostly level.

There is another SSS at 4.5 as the trail crosses a lichen-covered boulder drainage. I don't know exactly why, but I just love these types of places. I hope that you do too, because once we pass Deadman's Gap, we'll be hiking through them a lot. The trail eases uphill some, through mostly hardwoods, with a few scattered pines. There are a few views off to the right through the trees, especially during leaf-off.

Just before MILEPOST #5, there is another trail intersection. The spur up to the Panorama Vista on the Scenic Drive heads up the hill to the left. There is a pretty nice view from up there, if you're not in a hurry and have the energy. The main OT continues STRAIGHT AHEAD, on the level, to MILEPOST 5.0. From there it eases uphill just a little, then across a steep, rocky hillside, to another SSS area at 5.2— wonderful lichen-covered rocks and a great view.

From here the trail heads downhill some, past more views and steep, rocky hillside. The trail gets rather rocky in places too, which makes for tricky footing, especially when it's covered with leaves. The Scenic Drive can be seen in places just up the hill to the left. We've been paralleling it for a while now. At 5.7 the trail heads uphill some, swinging back to the left. It levels off and comes to Forest Road (FR) #6010 at 5.8. The Scenic Drive is just off to the left. This is the highest point on this section, at 2140 feet. Go STRAIGHT ACROSS the forest road and into the woods.

The trail heads downhill to the right, then swings back to the left. It goes through a number of "waves" of rock fields as it switchbacks down, passing MILEPOST #6. It levels off at 6.4, an SSS area of rocks and a great view. You can see Bohannon Lake in the distance. The trail quickly heads downhill again, through a nice rock formation that has some trees growing out of it. There are a couple of SSS views beyond as the trail continues down. It runs along an old roadbed for a short distance, past MILEPOST #7, then crosses another roadbed, and levels off for a bit.

Just past a seep, there is a trail intersection with a path that goes on down to Bohannon Lake (the trail may or may not be maintained). There was a rotting trail sign here when I came through (recently reported as not being there at all). The OT continues TO THE LEFT, down the hill. Out in front of you during leaf-off you can see a low spot in the ridge—this is Deadman's Gap.

At 7.3 the trail crosses Bohannon Creek, an SSS. Lots of rock slides. This creek runs most of the year, and is the largest one that we've seen since leaving the State Park. Looks like a nice spot to spend some time exploring around. The trail heads on downstream to the right, then leaves it up the hill. It levels off and swings around to the left. It does some up-and-downing, across some smaller drainages, and past several modified "N" trees. Then is heads uphill a little steeper, past large pine trees, and comes to MILEPOST #8. Just beyond is Deadman's Gap on the Scenic Drive.

The trail crosses the Scenic Drive, and heads downhill to the right, then left, then right again. We are now on the north side of Winding Stair Mountain, and will see a lot of different stuff than we've been looking at. Although this is a much more moist side of the hill, which means lots and lots of wildflowers, ferns and lush vegetation, there will be less flowing water. In fact, between here and Winding Stair Campground, there are only a couple of reliable water sources all year, and one of those is Horsethief Springs.

There are some pretty difficult stretches on this side too—the trail gets *very rough and rocky*. In fact, as the trail goes through many rock gardens, there really is no trail tread at all—just rocks. One reason for this is the fact that an endangered snail, the slit-mouth snail, inhabits some of these rock gardens, and the Forest Service is not allowed to disturb the rocks. Re-routing the trail usually doesn't help, because there will just be another rock garden in the way. So be patient through these rocky areas, and watch out for snails!

*Note that due to numerous trail reroutes, the **mileposts** in this stretch may or may not be accurate, and in fact the mileposts move sometimes too! The mileages in my description were recalculated in 2012 after all the reroutes, but I have not noted all of the mileposts due to their fluid nature.*

The trail *lev*els a bit, passes through the orange-post fence line, and continues switchbacking down. It gets pretty rocky. And levels off. At 8.3 there is an SSS area on the right—a moss-covered boulder field stretching up the hillside. There are lots of briars, and the trail even veers down to the left to avoid a messy patch. Then there's a smaller SSS area of moss-covered rocks that the trail goes down the middle of. We'll see lots of this type of trail on this side of the mountain. In some spots the trail is dug down into the rocks several feet—impressive trail work. Just imagine how much work it took. But then there are lots of other places where there weren't any rocks removed (because of the snails), and there really isn't much of a trail. This makes it hard to follow at times. Be sure to keep a watch out for the blue blazes, and in some places, rock cairns that have been built to help out.

We come to a trail intersection at 8.7. This is where we pick up the Boardstand Trail. It takes off to the left, and runs on down the hill and connects with the Military Road Trail (all blazed WHITE), which, of course, connects to the OT back at mile .7. This would make a good weekend loop, but keep in mind that there is a lot of elevation gain and loss along the way. I have not hiked it.

From the intersection, the OT continues STRAIGHT AHEAD. It drops down the hill a little on an old roadbed, through the barbed-wire fence again (until they fix it, this is a bad spot because of the wire). Soon after, the trail leaves the road TO THE RIGHT—be on the lookout for this. It heads up some, then a little bit level, then down steeply. Lots of rocks. You will hear this a lot—*Lots of rocks*. It levels off and crosses a drain, then runs through another boulder field—neat moss on the rocks. There are some monster oak trees through here too. Nice section, but rocky and difficult to walk on at times.

There are spotty views though the trees during leaf-off of the Holson River Valley and the hills beyond. Not any really spectacular views for a while, but you do have the feeling that you are on top of a pretty good ridge, which, of course, you are. This is all still Winding Stair Mountain.

As the trail goes up a slight hill, you pass MILEPOST #9. There is an off-trail SSS area down on the left, that you may be able to see through the trees. This is what I call a "Rock Glacier." We'll get to hike through several of them up ahead. I find that there is a difference between these "glaciers," "boulder fields," "rock gardens," and plain old "rock fields." Out West in the Rockies I would probably call all of them "scree fields" or something like that. But here, there are different types. The "glaciers" seem to me to be fresher that the other rock fields, usually lighter in color, and don't have much heavy lichen or moss growth on them. I can imagine them moving on down the hill over time, just like a glacier. Anyway, there's one down on the left.

(look for Rock Garden Shelter at 9.4) The trail levels off, does some up-and-downing through small drains, and passes by more wonderful oak trees, and crosses a wooden foot bridge. And there are lots and lots of rocks. *Lots of rocks.* It heads uphill some, crosses an old road trace, then more short and steep pitches up and down. At 9.7 there is a neat SSS area that I noted on the tape as being "weird." I guess you could say that the hillside has character—lots of little hills and ravines.

There are more rock garden areas, ups and downs, and a few drainages, even a little water in the wet season, with another wooden bridge at 10.1. It always seems that the uphill runs are steeper than the downhill ones. Then it's back down again, then up. Be careful through here since the trail is *very* rocky, and difficult to locate in some places. One trick that I use when there is no apparent trail tread, is to look ahead for an open corridor through the trees, as well as looking for the blazes. Take your time. And enjoy the rock gardens.

The trail continues across many small, dry, rocky drainages. Up and down. During a heavy rain, many of these little drains would be running and really neat. There wasn't much water in them when I came through. At 10.6 the trail passes another rock glacier, this one smaller, but still an SSS. The trail crosses it on the down side—careful, there is no tread, and these rocks may be slick when wet (I did a face plant here—a humbling experience when carrying a heavy backpack!). The footing, in fact, gets even worse ahead, as the trail heads up the hill some. It passes another glacier area on the left, then levels. Watch for paint blazes.

There is some normal trail for a while, with more ups and downs. Lots of huckleberry too— a welcome sight. At 11.1 we turn right onto a road trace for just a little ways, then exit it to the right. We head on over to a branch of Cedar Branch at 11.2. (This might be your last water until Winding Stair Campground.) This is a neat area during high water because the stream tumbles so steep. Right after we cross the stream we turn and head *steeply* down beside it. There is a waterfall along the way, and the whole area is an SSS. We soon turn away from the stream to the right, through a rock garden and then level off.

More rocks, a little up and downing across a steep hillside, with a general downward trend for the next half mile, leveling off and going across several small drainages. Then the trail curves back to the right and heads steeply up the hill—a trend that will continue for a while, sorry! Lots and lots of boulders in the trail tread and surrounding landscape—nice rock gardens all around.

More uphill, some of it steep, some not so steep. Lots of rocks. There are a couple of trail switchbacks, more uphill, then some level trail. Still more rocks, more up and downing, although not as tough a climb now, with a few level areas across several small creeks. The trail eases downhill a little bit to and across a fire road at 12.5, then runs level for a while, to another small creek in the 13.0 mile area—you cross this creek and glacier in three parts, then head downhill to the left after the 3rd crossing, then quickly level off back to the right, still in the glacier. I love these rock glaciers!

There is more up and downing across a couple of glaciers and also through some nice open woods. There is an SSS at 13.4 where the trail joins an old road that has been dug out through a large rock glacier, and follows the road for a little bit. The trail soon leaves the road and eases up the hill, then begins to head downhill a little bit and comes to a creek and SSS area at 13.9. This is what I call a "hump" glacier—the creek is split in two with a hump of rocks in between. This little creek eventually flows into Wildhorse Creek far below.

On the other side of the creek the trail turns to the right and heads uphill, then veers to the left, then back right again and levels out some. Lots of big pines, and some good campsites too.

The trail climbs on *up*, across a steep hillside that will take it out of you, then levels off some through more rock gardens and tricky footing. Then it is uphill again, through a couple of switchbacks, then more level. There is a good campsite in a low area here, then the trail heads uphill once again.

The trail heads downhill a little, then quickly levels off. This is a neat area, an SSS. Big trees. And boulders. And not too far beyond, the trail drops down and levels out in another SSS area of big pines, big boulders, and two sink holes on the right. These are depressions in the forest floor that are a conduit for water to enter caves deep below. There are some more great campsites in this area too.

The trail soon heads quickly up out of the area, then back down some, then level. The trail has been dug out real well through the next boulder field. It took lots of work. You can see the rest of the glacier up on the hillside to the right. There are several huge oaks in this area too—right along the trail. Lots of giant oaks and rock gardens. If your pack is not too heavy, and you are not too tired, all of this is an SSS.

Soon the trail switchbacks up the hill a couple of times, heads across a very steep hillside, then comes to a wonderful SSS glacier with spectacular view at 15.0. This is one of the longest views that you will see on the OT. More big oaks too. Soon the trail is running level again, and the hillside is not so steep, but there are still tons of rocks.

There are a few short switchbacks up, but nothing too major, as the trail passes MILEPOST #16. When I was last here (in July), *everything* on the ground was covered with Virginia creeper There is some decent trail ahead. It runs along the outside edge of a bench here and there. The leaf-off views are OK. Then more rock fields, and lots of little switchbacks up. Did I mention that there were lots of rocks? We are gradually climbing the hillside. At 16.8 there is a minor trail intersection—there is a spur trail that runs to the right, on up to the Scenic Drive. There isn't a parking area there, and it isn't even marked on the Scenic Drive anymore. (look for Holson Valley Vista Shelter at 16.8)

The OT continues STRAIGHT AHEAD, and drops down the hill a little, down to the Holson Valley Vista at 16.9. This is another terrific view out across the Ouachitas. The trail turns right here and continues down the hill a little, through more boulder fields, past MILEPOST #17. It switchbacks down some, then up some, past a few larger boulders, up some more, and close to the orange highway fence once again. We will be seeing a lot of this fence line from now on for a while. And in fact, will come right alongside it here and there.

The switchbacks are numerous, but short. Most of them are up, but a few are down. There is even some good trail, and a stand of pines, which we haven't seen too many of for a while. Just after a long downhill switchback, we pass MILEPOST #18. Back into hardwoods again we go, and more downhill switchbacks. And some level, rocky areas, and even some huckleberry, which we haven't seen in a while either.

At 18.7 there is a major trail intersection. The Horsethief Springs Trail goes to the left five miles down to Cedar Lake (also called the Cedar Lake Trail). You can also use this trail to loop back to the OT at 20.1, but it's a tough hike—the Forest Service has a free map showing all of this. A short spur heads steeply up the hill to the right to the Scenic Drive (both trails are blazed white). The OT continues STRAIGHT AHEAD. It goes up and down, past MILEPOST #19, then up again. Lots more pines, huckleberry, and up-and-downing.

For some reason, you will also see lots of "N" trees throughout this section. Since these trees are formed when other, larger trees fall across them when they are young (causing them to alter the direction of their growth until the fallen tree rots away), I guess this area has had lots of storms that knocked down trees. Hum.

The trail continues across a steep hillside, and passes a couple of narrow SSS rock glaciers at 19.3. The footing is pretty good here, even through the rocks. It is gradually working its way up the hillside, up to the spur trail to Horsethief Springs at 19.9. This is a great spot to drop your pack (or take it with you for a picnic) and take the spur trail up to the right to the picnic area at the old spring (which could be dry—it is no longer a reliable water source). There are a couple of tables, the old spring (which is enclosed with a neat rock structure) and toilets. This is one of the major stopping points on the Scenic Drive. Legend has it that outlaws from way back (namely Belle Starr) stopped here to water their stolen horses. NOTE: *THE SPRING MAY BE DRY!*

The OT continues STRAIGHT AHEAD, on the level, and soon crosses the outlet to the spring. Just beyond is MILEPOST #20.

At 20.1 there is another trail intersection. The trail down and to the left is a horse trail, and heads on down and connects with the trail to Cedar Lake. The trail up and to the right is blazed yellow and white, and is the Billy Creek West Trail (also goes to horse corrals). This trail was constructed to create a loop trail with the Billy Creek Trail, which connects with the OT ahead at 22.4. From Horsethief Springs, you can travel one of two loop possibilities to return to the OT (loops back to Horsethief Springs are 7.9 or 11.9 miles in length), or travel to Billy Creek Campground. The Forest Service has a free map of this.

The OT continues STRAIGHT AHEAD, some level, some gradual uphill. It passes an almost rock glacier, but doesn't go through it, so the footing is pretty good. In fact, most of the trail now for a while is in pretty good shape. Yea! It does more up-and-downing, runs alongside the orange fence (and very near the Scenic Drive), and past MILEPOST #21. There are a number of "N" trees a ways beyond—must have been a violent storm here way back when. Then the trail goes through a grove of cedar trees, and down to and across FR #6014 at 21.7. This road goes to Cedar Lake.

The trail crosses the road at an angle, then drops down the hill a little. There may be some open views through this area, perhaps even an SSS, but it was pretty foggy when I came through. The trail runs level for a while, past MILEPOST #22. There are mostly hardwoods through most of this, but there are a few big pines around, and even a pine grove or two. The trail is near the top of the ridge.

At 22.4 there is another trail intersection. The Billy Creek Trail takes off to the right, crosses the Scenic Drive, and heads down the south side of the mountain to the Billy Creek Campground. It connects with the Billy Creek West Trail for the loop back to the OT at Horsethief Springs that we passed earlier.

The OT continues STRAIGHT AHEAD. It begins to switchback up the hill a number of times, where it comes alongside an SSS ridge of rock—pretty nice formations. And also down to the left (at the first switchback), out through the woods a ways, there is an off-trail SSS—a large rock glacier, one of the best we've seen, but you have to get off of the trail to see it very well.

The trail continues to climb, up through lots of rocks, leveling off for a moment at 22.9 where there is a trail intersection. An unmarked spur goes to the left, on down and out to a terrific SSS view. In fact, this is one of the only spots on the OT that I know of that has a great, open view of the sunset. You'll find a boulder field there on the left—you have to go down a little to see the view. Nice spot. Definitely worth a look see. The Mountain Top Trail goes to the right at the intersection, and is blazed white. This loop trail begins at Winding Stair Campground, and utilizes part of the OT ahead to make a 2.2 mile loop. The OT from this point on to the Winding Stair Trailhead will be blazed both blue and white.

The main trail continues STRAIGHT AHEAD at this intersection, then heads up the hill some more and to the right, past MILEPOST #23. It goes up just a tad more, then levels off on the top of the ridge.

The forest floor is thick with huckleberry, and there are lots of great camp spots here. We are actually up above the Scenic Drive for the first time.

Soon it begins to head down on the south side of the hill, swinging back and forth. It levels some now along the north side of the hill, intersects an old road trace and follows it for a short distance, then leaves it to the right. It eases uphill some, then level, past a rock chimney on the left at 23.3. At the chimney there is a trail to the right—blazed white—that is a cutoff spur that goes on over across the Scenic Drive and connects to the return loop of the Mountain Top Trail. It is for those from the campground that want to shorten the loop trail. Just beyond this intersection is an SSS tree—a "double N" pine. You'll just have to see for yourself to figure it out. The trail remains mostly level, some gradual up-and-downing, past another "N" tree, staying near the ridgetop.

At 23.7 we come out to the Winding Stair Trailhead area (there is a big sign on the Scenic Drive). Be sure to register at the box. The parking area and the white-blazed Mountain Top Trail to the campgrounds are on the left. There is a bathroom, then a small Backpacker Campground, then the spur trail continues onto the main campground and to Emerald Vista on the other side of the main campground. The OT does not go through either campground.

This trailhead is a good place to access the trail, dump your trash, get water (may be turned off in the winter), camp, and use the facilities. *Please note—the campgrounds may be closed during the winter months, and there is NO WATER there during this time.*

Back at the registration box, the OT follows the forest road TO THE RIGHT, on out to and across the Scenic Drive. This is the end of Section One. Congratulations—you've made it (we hope) through the roughest section of the OT!

SECTION TWO—27.9 miles
Winding Stair Campground to Queen Wilhelmina Park

Trail Point	Mile Point	Mileage West to East	Mileage East to West
Winding Stair	23.7	0.0	27.9
Winding Stairs Shelter	25.0	1.3	26.6
Rough Mountain	27.0	3.3	24.6
FR #6023	28.3	4.6	23.3
Red Spring	28.4	4.7	23.2
Big Cedar Creek	30.3	6.6	21.3
Hwy. 259	30.5	6.8	21.1
Pashubbe Shelter	34.0	10.3	17.6
Pashubbe Trailhead	34.3	10.6	17.3
Wilton Mountain	36.7	13.0	14.9
Kiamichi River, #1 (western most crossing)	40.9	17.2	10.7
Kiamichi River, #8	43.1	19.4	8.5
Arkansas State Line	46.3	22.6	5.3
State Line Shelter	46.4	22.7	5.2
Pioneer Cemetery	49.5	25.8	2.1
Queen Wilhelmina State Park Lodge	51.6	27.9	0.0

Section Two is the longest on the OT. It begins in the WSNRA, passes through a short stretch of the Indian Nations National Scenic and Wildlife Area, runs down the middle of the Upper Kiamichi Wilderness Area, then crosses into Arkansas and ends at Queen Wilhelmina State Park. It crosses the Scenic Drive right at the beginning, then remains on the south side of Winding Stair and Rich mountains (climbing the latter).

The trail is all located on the Ouachita National Forest (except the last little part). All of this section in Oklahoma is on the Kiamichi Ranger District, but is managed by the Choctaw Ranger District (office located in Heavener). The part of the trail in Arkansas is located on the Mena Ranger District. Their office is in Mena. Quads are Big Cedar and Page, Oklahoma; Mountain Fork, Ark-Okla; and Rich Mountain, Arkansas (just the last tiny bit).

Generally speaking, the trail is in better condition here on the south side of the mountains, there is more flowing water (the trail is usually lower in elevation), but the hillsides are drier, with less wildflowers. There are a lot of access points along the way, so you can hike short stretches if desired. An abundance of scenery!

This is an easier stretch to hike than Section One was. There are a couple of pretty good climbs in the beginning, then it heads down

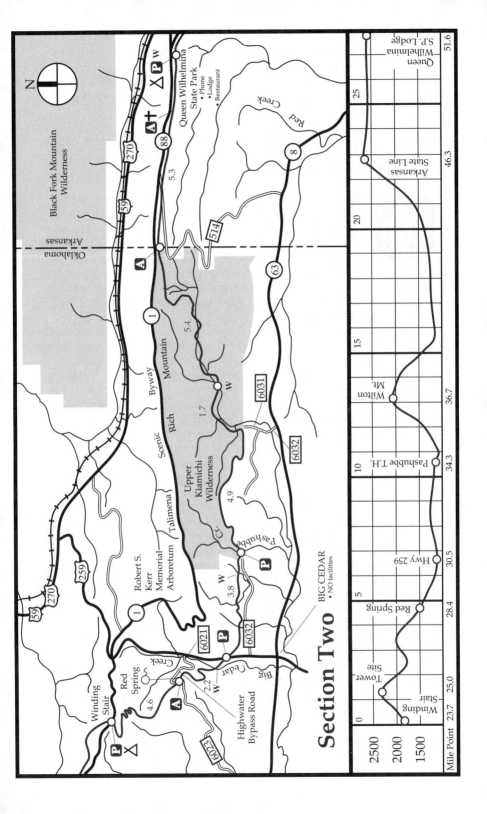

Section Two

BIG CEDAR
• NO facilities

Queen Wilhelmina S.P. Lodge

Arkansas State Line

Wilton Mt.

Pashubbe T.H.

Hwy 259

Red Spring

Tower Site

Winding Stair

2500											
2000											
1500											

Mile Point 23.7 25.0 28.4 30.5 34.3 36.7 46.3 51.6

0   5   10   15   20   25

Black Fork Mountain Wilderness

Queen Wilhelmina State Park
• Phone
• Lodge
• Restaurant

Red Creek

Oklahoma
Arkansas

Rich Mountain

Scenic Byway (Talimena)

Upper Kiamichi Wilderness

Robert S. Kerr Memorial Arboretum

Winding Stair

Red Spring

Big Cedar Creek

Highwater Bypass Road

Pashubbe

270 59 88 270

59 1

514 63 8

6031 6032

6021 6032 6023

1 259

5.3
5.4
1.7
4.9
3.8
2.2
4.6

N

Winding Stair Mountain, crosses Big Cedar Creek, and heads over to the wilderness area. It crosses the Kiamichi River a bunch of times, then makes a tough climb up Rich Mountain, and remains mostly level to the end of the section. There is usually plenty of water, except for the last six miles or so.

The trailhead is located on the Scenic Drive, right next to Winding Stair Campground (there is a separate sign and entrance for each on the Scenic Drive), which is just west of Hwy. 259. **The campground is closed during the winter months.**

 The trail leaves the parking area and heads back out the entrance road to the Scenic Drive. This is mile 23.7. It crosses the highway, continues up a dirt road on the other side (the Mountain Top Trail takes off to the right, and is blazed white), swinging to the left a little, just for a short distance, then leaves the road TO THE RIGHT at a gate. The trail wanders around up a rocky hillside at a pretty good clip, and intersects with a closed road. TURN RIGHT on this road and continue up the hill. MILEPOST #24 is just beyond.

And I do mean *up* the hill. Although this is a nice, smooth walk along the old road, it is a long, steady climb. Eventually the road does level off somewhat, as it swings around to the left at 24.5. There are some pretty good views here out over the treetops. The trail enters the Indian Nations National Scenic & Wildlife Area at this point, and is in the area for the next four miles or so, then heads back into the WSNRA.

This next little bit is a wonderful hike—smooth, wide and level trail, still on the old road. It soon eases up just a little, and tops out at the old Winding Stair Fire Tower site (also known as the "Billy" Tower). All that are left are the concrete pilings of the tower. Someone has added a huge rock cairn to signify that this spot is the highest point on the Ouachita Trail so far at 2,451 feet. With the elevation comes a terrific SSS view, and MILEPOST #25. (look for Winding Stairs Shelter 25.0)

From the tower site, the trail heads over the edge to the right, then quickly left, and begins to make its way down the ridgeline. There are wonderful SSS views all along the way for a while. And even a rock glacier at 25.2. It's pretty darn good trail too, as it heads down the hill. Eventually the trail swings around the point to the left, and more great views. Then it begins an incredible switchbacking drop down to a saddle—there are 33 switchbacks in all!

MILEPOST #26 is right after the 23rd turn. But I must say, the trail is excellent, there are gobs of large pines, and more good views. You can keep an eye on your progress as you go down by looking at the hills around you—at first you are above them, but gradually they begin to grow, and you end up looking *up* at them. Thirty-three switchbacks. Gosh, I'm glad we're hiking this thing in this direction. The hill right in front is Rough Mountain, which is where the trail goes next.

There is a good campsite in the saddle at 26.3, but no water, unless you explore either of the drainages that head up at this spot. The trail goes through the saddle and heads uphill, and begins to switchback through several rocky areas. The lichen-covered boulders at 26.5 are an SSS. The footing is pretty good, not too rocky. As the trail continues up Rough Mountain, there is a great open view back to the big hill that we just came down. You can see a number of those rock glaciers that I've been raving about. They come pretty far down the hillside.

The trail swings on around the hill to the left, levels off, and passes MILEPOST #27. Then it curves to the right and heads down a ridgetop. It wanders back and forth along it, generally heading downhill, but some level too. Right at MILEPOST #28 there is a small rock outcrop and an SSS view out across Hwy. 259, over Coon Mountain to Rich Mountain, which we will get to climb up in a few miles. There are plenty of good campsites in this area, and lots of level trail. At 28.3 we cross FR #6023 on an angle to the left, and continue into the woods. We re-enter the WSNRA at this point, and remain in it until crossing into the Upper Kiamichi Wilderness Area near the Pashubee Trailhead.

[*HIGHWATER BYPASS. If things are flooded you may want to consider hiking forest roads from this point down to the highway. TURN LEFT onto FR #6023 and follow it downhill, eventually connecting with FR #K35C (to the left), and then TURN RIGHT onto FR #6021. (You still have to cross the creek THREE TIMES before getting to Hwy. 259 though, so this may still be dangerous.) Then TURN RIGHT and follow the highway south to the trailhead.*]

From FR #6023 the trail heads downhill and turns left. At the next turn to the right at 28.4 there is an intersection. The little spur heads on over to the left about 50 feet to Red Spring, which is a good water source most of the year, but can dry up once in a while. The water tasted a lot better than Horsethief Springs did, but the ground around it is getting pretty red from all the iron. It's just another one of Mother Nature's paint brushes.

The OT continues TO THE RIGHT, easing down the hill across a steep, rocky hillside. There are lots of big pines, and a few larger hardwoods too. There is one area of thick underbrush, it even got a little dark while I went through it, then all of a sudden the woods opened up and all was bright again.

The hillside gets really steep now, as the trail swings around the nose of it to the right, dropping slightly, past MILEPOST #29. Just beyond that is a wonderful SSS rock glacier—one of the best on the trail. It's narrow, but goes all the way down to the creek below, and quite a ways above too. I love this spot. The trail goes right through it on large rocks, and drops on down the hill to a neat SSS stream at 29.2. There are lots of large, moss-covered boulders and ferns here. Reminds me of the Ozark Highlands Trail. It crosses the stream and curves back to the left. Soon you can look over and see the rock glacier straight on through the trees. At one spot here the trail is thickly lined with ferns on both sides.

The trail leaves the creek area and swings back to the right, uphill just slightly, around the nose of a ridge, then level, and down some. It goes through another thicket of pines and across a small drain. Soon you can hear the rushing waters of Big Cedar Creek. Across another drain, then alongside the creek itself at 29.9. The trail used to cross Big

Cedar at this spot (for a total of three crossings), but a new re-route will take us on downstream before we do (only one crossing now). There is a campsite at this spot, and I would call the area an SSS—there are lots of things down along the creek covered with moss.

The trail continues straight ahead along the creek downstream, looking down on it at times. It swings away from it a little, across a flat, to a seep area that is guarded by a couple of big hardwoods, an SSS. This is MILEPOST #30. From here the trail stays mostly level, next to the creek some, and at 30.2 comes out to a registration box—please sign in (this is where the old section of trail used to come in from the left). The creek out through the bushes is pretty nice with all the boulders in it—an SSS.

Back at the box, the trail picks up an old road trace and follows it on over to the crossing of Big Cedar Creek at 30.3. This is one of the largest water crossings that we'll make on the OT. You can often cross dry here by hopping across on the rocks, but you will sometimes have to wade too, as I did this March day. (This water, as well as the rest of the streams from here to the Arkansas line, all eventually drain into the Red River, which forms part of the Texas/Oklahoma border.) Once across, follow the old road on out to Big Cedar Trailhead—Hwy. 259 is just beyond.

This highway has special meaning for me. One of my heroes, John F. Kennedy, dedicated it back in 1961, at the community of Big Cedar, just a mile down the road (there is a small memorial to him there). This road is also the dividing line between Winding Stair Mountain, which we've been traveling along for the past 30 miles, and Rich Mountain, which we will be with for the next 26 miles, all the way to Hwy. 270 at mile 56.7.

From the trailhead, follow the road out to and across the highway at 30.5, pick up an old road trace on the other side, and TURN RIGHT onto it. This is a wide, level walk through a pine forest. There is one nice big oak that leans out over the trail. At 30.7 a powerline comes in from the left, and the trail follows it straight ahead. Not too far beyond, about in the middle of the powerline section at 30.8, the trail leaves it TO THE LEFT, and heads up into the woods on plain trail.

It winds around on up a little, past MILEPOST #31, then eases down some through a nice cedar thicket. It crosses a couple of little creeks, then eases up the hill to a frog-choked pond at 31.4. From there it drops down to and across another small creek, then another one at 31.6, an SSS area with some good camping nearby. This is another Ozark-type stream!

The trail turns to the left, heads uphill, and begins to switchback up a ridge. This is actually the lower flanks of part of Rich Mountain. We won't get to climb the real thing until about mile 45.0. It crosses an old road trace, passes MILEPOST #32 right after, and continues to climb up the ridge. It soon tops out, runs across the ridge to another wildlife pond on the left at 32.2, then begins to drop down the other side, swinging right, then left on an old road trace. There is another pond soon that the trail runs right alongside of.

It continues to drop down some, across a tiny creek, picks up an old road trace to the right, and heads out through an old clear-cut area that is growing up thickly with pines. I am so glad that the Forest Service has the trail corridor protected from future clear-cuts. We lost some valuable trail here in the Ouachitas, as well as in the Ozarks, due to clear-cuts. Anyway, the trees are growing up nicely now.

The trail stays mostly level, quickly leaves the road trace, goes through an area of larger pines, and down to and across a larger SSS stream at 32.8 (nice campsite too). There are lots of rock gardens along here, many of them moss-covered. It crosses a smaller stream, and enters another pine plantation, swinging to the left and up the hill, past MILEPOST #33. (My lucky number. Some idiot had already swiped the post though.) These trees were about 10–15 feet tall in 1993.

The trail swings left and right as it continues up the hill at a pretty good clip, then levels off and drops down to and across a lesser forest road at 33.2. It drops a little more, across another lesser road, then heads down (back into hardwoods) and across another small stream. There is a neat little stream a little ways beyond, with a miniature rock slough just upstream.

The trail eases uphill a tad, then runs level to and across a third forest road at 33.5. It bumps up, then does some up-and-downing across a couple of small streams, under a powerline, and down to another little SSS stream. (look for Pashubee Shelter at 34.0) It passes MILEPOST #34, easing up slightly, across another small stream, and out level across an old road trace to a corner of the 10,819 acre Upper Kiamichi River Wilderness Area on the left. We will be hiking the boundary (there are signs) from now on for a few miles, then will walk right through the middle of it. A little ways beyond at 34.3 is the Pashubbe Trailhead. This area is a giant flat, with room to camp a very large group. This trailhead is at the end of FR #6032—Hwy. 259 is three miles to the right. The turnoff to it is just south of the Big Cedar Trailhead.

At this point we leave the WSNRA. We will still be in the Ouachita National Forest, all the way to the other side of Hwy. 9, which is at 191.8. The only break is to go through Queen Wilhelmina State Park for a few miles.

Also at this point there is an old trail (Pashubbe Trail) that takes off to the north from the trailhead and eventually climbs *up* to the Scenic Drive on Rich Mountain. This was built by the game department to be used for hunter access, and is not used very much, or maintained. I am told that there is an incredible waterfall just about a mile up it, which is pretty easy to get to, before the trail really gets into the meat of the mountain. It's a terraced waterfall, that plunges into a wonderful pool 8–10 feet deep. If you are camping here, you might want to check it out.

From the trailhead, the OT heads down some steps and quickly levels out in the bottom at a registration box (do what there???). It crosses several rocky streams, normally OK, but could get tricky during high water. These creeks together are Pashubbe Creek. We continue to follow along the boundary of the wilderness area, as you can see by the endless numbers of signs. The trail forms the boundary all the way to the Kiamichi River Trailhead.

There is a clear-cut area on the right that is growing up nicely, as the trail turns to the left and heads uphill. It passes an American holly tree on the left—the first that I remember seeing on this trail. This is a beautiful evergreen species, with thorny leaves. Makes me think of Christmas. The trail gets a bit steep, and there is a nice view back behind. It levels off past a wildlife pond on the right at 34.8 (reliable water source if the creek is dry), heads uphill some more, swinging left and right, past MILEPOST #35. We are making our way up a rocky ridge line, still following those darn signs.

Soon the trail turns to the right and levels out somewhat, across a very steep hillside. There are some spotty views out through the trees during leaf-off, out across the Kiamichi River Valley. There is a small rock glacier SSS at 35.6. Most of the trail through here is in good shape, but it's a little rocky through that spot. From there the trail heads uphill, swinging back to the left, then right as it tops out on a briar-patch ridge at 35.8.

It follows along the top of the ridge past MILEPOST #36. Lots of huckleberry and moss. There is a view or two through the trees during leaf-off of a pretty good hill up ahead—this is Wilton Mountain, an offshoot of Rich Mountain. The trail begins to head *up* the hill at a good clip. This is a steep, steep climb up the rocky hillside. It swings to the right and pauses for a minute at 36.4 beside a large rock for a nice view, then resumes the climbing and turns back and forth across the ridgeline. It passes an SSS area of larger boulders, and finally does top out at 36.7.

Once on top the trail turns to the right, and although it is pretty rocky, the level trail is a welcome relief. Good campsite, if you want to haul water up. And the views during leaf-off are nice both east and west. You get a good look into the main part of the Upper Kiamichi Wilderness Area.

The trail heads on down the ridgetop—some rocky footing, some good. It passes MILEPOST #37, then levels off a bit. More downhill, and at 37.8 there is an SSS spot of rock outcrops and a nice view. I guess you can look out across the wilderness and see Arkansas off yonder. That's great, but we're going to have to work to get there. (The trail crosses the state line on *top* of Rich Mountain.) The trail picks its way up through the rocky area, on the right side of the ridge now, then begins to drop off that side past MILEPOST #38.

There are several big switchbacks down just ahead, mostly good trail, past giant pine trees and a couple of SSS views. At 38.3 the trail goes through a tiny saddle and picks up a road trace. Just beyond, the trail leaves the trace TO THE RIGHT, goes through a dry drainage, past a property corner, then rejoins the road trace again—TURN RIGHT and follow the road. There is a wonderful, open SSS view just beyond out through the great pines. And then the road begins to head down the hill. You can tell it has been a while since this road was used because there are some pretty good sized trees growing right in the middle of it.

You will see lots of red paint on the trees in some places. This used to mark private property, but it is all National Forest land now. Yea! They try to acquire land within wilderness areas whenever possible, sometimes even trading other lands on the edge of the forest.

It passes through a small field at 38.8, an SSS view area, then heads downhill a little steeper, to another opening, where it curves back to the right. This point is one of the best views yet on the entire trail. You can look deep into the wilderness, and the mountains beyond. One ridge after another after another. During leaf-off you can even see a river below—this is the Kiamichi River. We will get to know it intimately in a little while. Ahh yes, wilderness areas sure are nice.

Soon the old road turns back to the left, and you get a good view of the hand of man—you can't even walk in the road because it's washed out so deep. MILEPOST #39 is just beyond. Past the MILEPOST the trail goes through a fence line, leaves the roadbed, and drops down steeply to another old road trace—TURN RIGHT on this and follow it on the level.

The trail continues along the old road trace—we'll be on this old road for quite a while. In fact, we'll be on one old road or another for most of the next five miles. It's a level, easy walk, although there are many spots that get quite rocky, and rather soupy during the wet season. It crosses four small drains, then comes alongside the Kiamichi River at 39.5, running along it for a while. Then it veers away from it, still on the road trace. There are lots of campsites around. Just beyond the next creek crossing is MILEPOST #40.

The trail passes through an old field, crosses several more small creeks, and comes to a trail intersection at 40.5. There is a side road that goes to the right over to the river. The OT continues STRAIGHT AHEAD on the road trace. It goes through a stretch of clay/mud that isn't much fun, and remains mostly level. Just as the road curves to the left a little, the trail LEAVES THE ROAD TO THE RIGHT—follow the blazes. The road ahead is more grown up, so you shouldn't have too much trouble noticing this turn. The trail runs on across a flat (and a tiny stream), and comes to our first of fifteen crossings of the Kiamichi River at 40.9.

During normal wet seasons, this would be a wet crossing, as are some of the others ahead. During drier seasons, you could probably hop across on rocks (this is a two-part crossing). There is certainly water here all year. Since we have so many crossings up ahead, and the trail is so easy, what I did was to put on my tennis shoes here, and just leave them on for a few miles until I could make the crossings dry. When I hike, I usually get after it at a pretty good pace, and don't want to be bogged down with time-consuming footwear changing/drying at creek crossings.

On the other side of that coin, water is magical, and all of these river crossings are special. So take the time to pause, rest up, and take a close look around you at all the wonderful things at your feet. (Changing your shoes and drying your feet is a great excuse to stop and smell the flowers.) This spot is an SSS. The river is lined with witch-hazel bushes, which come to life during sunny winter days, and will knock you over with the scent of their blooms.

Once across the river, the trail crosses another stream, then curves to the left, upstream but away from the river, through a level area on plain trail. It passes MILEPOST #41, crosses the small stream again, and continues across the flat area, then comes alongside the river. This whole area is probably under water during a big flood, so I wouldn't recommend hiking it then. There are a number of small streams weaving here and there.

At 41.2 we cross the river the second time. I had to wade it. And in fact had a near disaster here—I dropped my tape recorder into the river. I fished it out, of course, and it continued to work, but the next couple miles of trail on the tape were somewhat garbled. I must say that I put my little Radio Shack recorder through many rough times, and it never completely failed me.

The trail crosses several smaller streams, and intersects with another old road trace at 41.5—TURN RIGHT and follow the road. More easy hiking, though it gets rocky at times. We are right up against the hillside on the left. It crosses a couple more drains, then comes to a two-part crossing of the river again at 41.9, crossing number three. I was able to find some rocks to hop across, but much more water and I would have gotten wet. Just beyond on the road, is MILEPOST #42.

The trail continues near the river, coming alongside it at 42.3, an SSS with boulders in the creek and big pines. And just beyond is our fourth river crossing, a wet one for me. The next crossing is at 42.7, and you can often hop across. And soon after that is the sixth crossing, where you'll find a few slick stepping stones. There is a stretch of trail beyond that is completely covered with a carpet of moss—pretty nice walking. And then MILEPOST #43, which is next to the river.

At 43.1 is the seventh river crossing, and just beyond is the eighth and *final* river crossing. You might be able to hop across on stones, but these will often be wet crossings. (If the water is very high, I would skip these two crossings and bushwhack up the stream between them.) The trail is still on the road, which is rocky in spots, but usually good footing, and even some more moss carpeting. It crosses a couple of small streams, and there is an occasional view of the river.

(Now begins a 2.6 mile reroute of the original trail. You should fill up with water before leaving the road—the river is just off to the right—you may not see water again for a long time. This new trail section is some of the worst designed and built that you will ever hike. It is difficult to follow at times, so be on the lookout for blazes. The new route is .8 of a mile longer than the original route, so you will have to add this mentally to your trip as the mileposts beyond the end of the reroute remain the same.)

At 43.8 the trail leaves the road TO THE LEFT and heads straight uphill, beginning a 1300+ foot descent up to the state line *(this is the new trail)*. It winds around a bit, then joins an old log road—TURN LEFT onto the road, going uphill. This old road heads very steeply up the hillside, passing MILEPOST #44 just before the road levels out (there may not be a milepost here since it is new trail).

The road does level off for a moment, then eases up some to 44.1 where you leave the road TO THE RIGHT onto plain trail. This takes you up a steep, rocky hillside where the trail winds around a bit, swings left, finally leveling off just below a small bluffline, which is just uphill to the right. This level trail does not last for long, as the trail turns right and heads straight up into the hillside and through the small bluffline. After it does this a couple of more times, the trail finally lands on top of a bluffline and curves back to the right, then continues along the outside edge of the hillside.

At 44.4 there is a pretty nice SSS view off to the right. Just beyond, the trail swings to the left and away from the view area, and joins an old log road, which heads uphill. It levels off and crosses a seep area, then continues uphill, first alongside and then on the old road. Near the top of the hill the road disappears and the trail curves to the right and continues as plain trail.

At 44.8 the trail goes through the right side of a nice, wide saddle, then curves to the right and runs along the left hand side of a narrow ridge. It dips down a bit, then switchbacks up the hillside a couple of times. There are some good leaf-off views out to the left through here. At MILEPOST #45 (may not be a milepost here) the trail hits the final switchback to the left, at the base of a small, rocky Razorback Ridge, which is just above the trail to the right.

The trail continues near the top of this ridge, and there are some SSS views off to the right, looking deep into the wilderness area. Some uphill trail, some mostly level. At 45.3 the trail goes through another saddle, then heads uphill again, and moves on over to the right side of the ridge. There are some nice leaf-off views.

There are a couple of quick switchbacks downhill at MILEPOST #46 (may not be a milepost here), then the trail crosses a wet-weather creek. There is an SSS downstream a bit to the right, and *surprise*, there is a WATERFALL! I have not been here when the falls were running, but there was water here during a dry August visit, so I expect there to be water here much of the year.

The next .8 miles of trail will be unofficial since the real MILEPOST #46 is .8 miles from this spot. This distance is the extra mileage of the reroute.

From the little creek the trail heads uphill, then drops back down, crossing the creek again a couple of times. It eases up the hill a bit, then levels off for a little while (the new trail rejoins the old trail here, but you will probably not notice it). Soon the trail heads up a very rocky hillside. At times there is no trail, only rocks to walk on, and then it passes the original MILEPOST #46 (actually at 46.8, but we will drop that extra .8 from our log from now on—you will just have to know that you hiked nearly an extra mile).

The trail is pretty straight now (but still up). It finally comes to a welcome sight—our old friends those orange highway posts. We go through the fence line and on up to a level spot (yes, I said level) at 46.3. This is the top of Rich Mountain, and the registration box there is at the Arkansas State Line. A little spur up to the left goes to the State Line

Parking Area (and a trash can) on the Scenic Drive. Although we might actually get a few feet higher along the ridge, I'm going to call this the highest point on the Ouachita Trail at 2610 feet.

(look for Stateline Shelter at 46.4)

The OT continues STRAIGHT AHEAD and enters the great State of Arkansas, The Natural State. It also leaves the Upper Kiamichi Wilderness Area at the line. You may see some signs here that mention Rich Mountain Tower. The OT does not go there, so don't pay any attention to them. The trail begins a pattern of running mostly level across the steep hillside, with some up-and-downing, and stays alongside, but just below and out of sight of, the Scenic Drive. The trail is in pretty good shape, although it gets rocky in a spot or two. Just past some big rock slabs is MILEPOST #47.

At 47.2 we see the first of many of what I call "wizard trees." These are stunted oak trees that remind me of those apple trees in the Wizard of Oz. An SSS. This is a pleasant walk through here. Eventually the trail drops down to and crosses FR #514 at 47.8 on an angle to the left. The trail remains mostly level, easing up some, past lots more wizard trees. It levels off some at MILEPOST #48. The Scenic Drive is just off to the left.

The underbrush gets kind of thick and nasty along here for a while—grown up with briars and such. We'll see this happen off and on for a while. I don't recommend hiking this section in shorts during the summer. Lots more wizard trees. At 48.4 we pass by a microwave tower that is on the left. (Did you bring any popcorn?) The trail dips down a little, then back up again, and runs right on top of the ridge. It crosses a ditch. More weeds. And wizard trees. Then heads down hill again, through a rocky section.

Right at MILEPOST #49 you can look down below the trail during leaf-off and see a nice rock glacier. There are more rocks on the trail too, with some tricky footing, but mostly level trail. We pass through a rock wall at 49.3, the first I've noticed on this trail. We head uphill some here, and pass through a couple more walls, to an SSS area lush with spring-fed grasses and stuff. Must have been a home site here somewhere.

From there the trail heads uphill some, then levels out. Lots of wizard trees. At 49.5 we come to the Pioneer Cemetery, a historical SSS, which is just on the left. It is circled by a split-rail fence. There is a parking area on the Scenic Drive just above. Although there are a number of graves, the writings on all but one of the headstones have weathered away. The story goes that a little girl who lived nearby many moons ago was chased up into a tree by wolves one night as she was gathering firewood. She froze to death up in the tree. She was the first one buried here.

There is a blue-blazed spur trail beyond the cemetery that goes up to the parking area—be sure not to take this trail, but continue STRAIGHT AHEAD on the OT. It heads downhill some, across a nearly rock-free hillside, crossing a wet spring area at 49.8, another SSS. Big trees. Lush grasses. From there the trail eases on up the hill a little, past MILEPOST #50.

Besides all of the wizard trees around, I saw several woodcocks right in the middle of the trail. This is a funny looking bird that you don't see very often in this part of the country. It looks a lot like a snipe, with its long beak. Of course, you hunt these birds with a shotgun, not a tote sack like you do snipes.

The trail is on an old road trace now, doing some up-and-downing, and passes another rock wall. Then it enters the boundary of Queen Wilhelmina State Park at 50.3 (there is a sign). We will get back into the Ouachita National Forest soon after leaving the State Park. Until then, camping is only permitted at the park campground, which we will hike right past.

Just beyond the boundary sign another nice rock wall comes down to and runs alongside the trail—an SSS. There is a spring soon after. The wall rejoins us again, and it is all a nice, pleasant hike. We pass by some old, rotted benches on the right at 50.6, then the trail dips down the hill and leaves the road trace to the left, levels out some, then rejoins the old road—TURN LEFT and continue uphill on the road. The underbrush is thick with heavy briars—not a good spot to wander off the trail.

The trail quickly swings up the hill, past a registration box, and comes out at the Scenic Drive at 50.9. TURN RIGHT here and head on over to the end of the campground (do *not* cross the Scenic Drive). Pick up pavement there, and continue along the sites, over a miniature railroad track, to MILEPOST #51, which is at campsite #29. Follow this road past the laundry building (outside telephone), a full-sized railroad engine, and a zoo to a parking lot on the left. Take the sidewalk that leaves the end of it on up around to the left . This takes you past an open view of the 13,579 acre Black Fork Mountain Wilderness Area across the way—a number of huge rock glaciers are visible on the hillside. When the sidewalk intersects with the road, TURN LEFT and go on around the north (left) side of the lodge. The elevation here is 2570 feet.

The trail continues on past the lodge, and leaves the pavement TO THE LEFT at a covered walkway at 51.6. This is also the beginning of the Lover's Leap Trail. I highly recommend that you take some time and tour the lodge building, have some lunch, and look at the views on the other side of the lodge. And if you really want a treat, get a room for the night. The windows are tiny, but the shower and bed sure do feel good. And I certainly recommend the "Ouachita Trail Breakfast," a western-style omelet. This is the end of Section Two, the longest section of the OT.

SECTION THREE—16.5 miles
Queen Wilhelmina State Park to Hwy. 71

Trail Point	Mile Point	Mileage West to East	Mileage East to West
Queen Wilhelmina State Park Lodge	51.6	0.0	16.5
Talimena Scenic Drive	54.1	2.5	14.0
Hwy. 270 Trailhead	56.7	5.1	11.4
Black Fork Mtn. Trail	57.8	6.2	10.3
Black Fork Mtn. Shelter	57.8 (+1)	6.3	10.4
Eagle Gap/Clear Fork	58.5	6.9	9.6
Unnamed Creek	67.7	16.1	.4
Foran Gap/Hwy. 71	68.1	16.5	0.0

Section Three is the shortest section on the OT. It begins at the State Park, but the rest of it is located on the Mena Ranger District of the Ouachita National Forest. Their office is on Hwy. 71 in Mena. Quads are Rich Mountain and Acorn. There are several access points in the first half of the section, but none for the rest of it until the end.

This is a pretty easy section to hike. The trail begins high on Rich Mountain, drops down the north side of it across the Ouachita River, climbs up a small part of Black Fork Mountain, drops down to Eagle Gap, then heads up a little and along the first long stretch of Fourche Mountain to Foran Gap at Hwy. 71. The first section of the trail on the south side of the Scenic Drive is in terrible condition, but the rest of the section is very good trail for the most part. Lots of good views.

Water is a problem after Eagle Gap—there basically isn't any from there until nearly Hwy. 71, which is over nine miles. And there are no access points along that stretch to stash any at either.

The trail access is at the Lodge at Queen Wilhelmina State Park, which is located up on Talimena Scenic Drive west of Mena. There is no separate parking area, but there is plenty of space. Be sure to check in at the Park office in the Lodge. The restaurant there is great, and welcomes OT hikers. There is a petting zoo and miniature railroad too, as well as a campground and other short hiking trails. And, of course, a spectacular view.

 The trail takes off from near the northeast corner of the Lodge building, at the Lover's Leap Trailhead shelter there, at OT mile 51.6. It heads down a flight of steps, across the miniature railroad tracks and into the woods. It is blazed both blue and yellow for a while. This first section is a wide, heavily used trail, with many wood steps. It drops down just a little, then rises up to the Lover's Leap Overlook at 51.8, of course, an SSS view. And a really nice one at that.

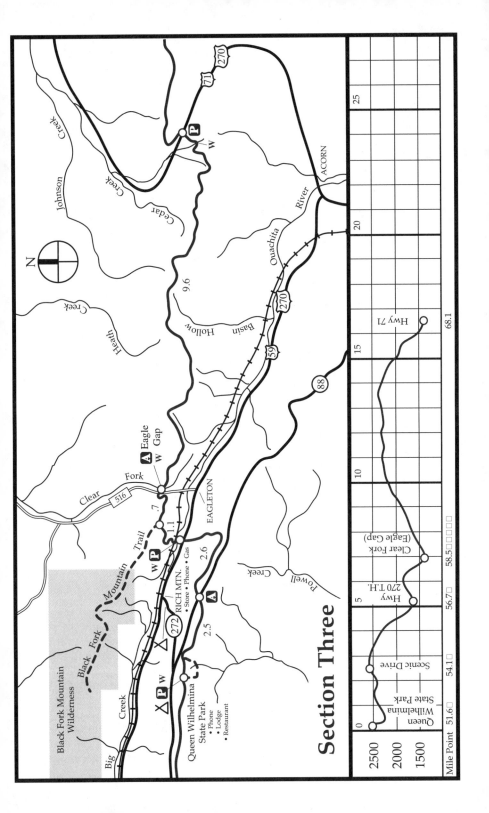

Section Three

The OT continues on, dropping again, past MILEPOST #52 (there may not be one here). Just beyond, the trail splits, and the Lover's Leap Trail goes to the right (loops back to the Lodge), and the OT TURNS LEFT. There is a headstone of all things there to mark the way (vandals kept tearing up the regular sign). The trail is regular width now as it switchbacks on down the hill. It is very rocky and the footing isn't too good. You should probably get used to this, because it's like that for a while.

The trail goes through a low area near the Scenic Drive, then curves to the right, away from it, and begins to climb. As it makes its way on around the hillside to the left, there is a nice SSS view at 52.5. The trail is steep and rocky in places, and doesn't really have much of a tread. It passes a narrow rock glacier, and a small spring. There is a level spot or two, but mostly uphill. And we are again graced with a bunch of wizard trees, which we haven't seen for a while.

Just as the trail gets ready to go around a small nose of a ridge (right after the old wash tub), we pass MILEPOST #53. The trail is mostly level now as it swings to the left, but very narrow. It eases uphill some, then level. And at 53.5, during leaf-off, you can look out ahead and see the Rich Mountain Tower, which we won't have to climb up to. It is up at 2681 feet, one of the highest points in Arkansas. By the way, just FYI, Rich Mountain likes to eat airplanes. There have been more than 50 crashes in the area.

The trail drops some, past more wizards, steeply for a little ways. Then it turns to the left and heads *very* steeply up the hill past MILEPOST #54. Just off to the right there is a wonderful SSS rock outcrop that will help to make up for the steep grade. It crosses the Scenic Drive at 54.1.

On the other side it drops down just a tad, turns to the right and runs level for a while along a level bench. We are now back on the north side of the mountain, and the vegetation is a little different. The trail is much better than it has been for a while. Soon it heads up the hill to the next bench, and levels off there. There are more wizard trees here, but they seem a little taller than they have been. Right at MILEPOST #55 is an SSS area of wizards, and a nice view across to the end of Black Fork Mountain.

There are a couple of big rocks next to the trail as it rises up just slightly, then begins to head down the hill. At 55.3 there is an SSS area of spring-fed mosses and ferns. And then another very narrow rock glacier, and lots of boulder fields. The trail is dug down into them pretty deep, so the footing is OK. Many, many wizards. And the trail continues downhill at a pretty good clip, switchbacking to the left, then the right, then left again, past MILEPOST #56. We are snaking back and forth across the top of a finger ridge, gradually making our way off Rich Mountain.

The grade gets less as we continue down the hill, into a pine forest, where we pick up an old road trace. At 56.3 we come alongside a neat stretch of rock wall that was made out of much smaller rocks than usual, an SSS. The road turns to the right some there, and we get more views of Black Fork Mountain out ahead of us—we'll be climbing part way up it in a little while.

The trail heads into an old grown up field area that seems impassable except for the trail as the road sort of disappears and the footing gets questionable. There is someone's house off in the woods to the right. We pick up a powerline and follow it past a registration box to Hwy. 270 at 56.7. It crosses the highway and enters the woods on the other side, swings to the left some, and goes over to the Black Fork Mountain Wilderness Trailhead at 56.8.

If you really want a treat, the Rich Mountain Country Store is about 1.3 miles up the highway to the west—they make wonderful ice cream shakes there, and have other goodies that taste like a million bucks, especially right after you come off of the trail! They also have a campground, little store, gas and *showers*. Hwy. 270 is the bottomland route through these hills to Oklahoma. It runs in the valley between Rich Mountain and Black Fork Mountain.

From the trailhead, the trail drops on down a small hill and crosses the Ouachita River on a nice bridge. This section of the trail for the next mile is also blazed with white paint, which marks the Black Fork Mountain Wilderness Trail that we share the tread with. On the other side of the river TURN RIGHT and follow a roadbed up onto a real railroad track. It crosses to the left into the woods.

The trail heads uphill some, picks up another road trace and levels off past MILEPOST #57. From there it soon leaves the roadbed and heads back up the hill TO THE RIGHT. This is part of Black Fork Mountain that we are heading up (we have left Rich Mountain behind). It swings back and forth on a steady grade, then levels out to the right past a surveyor's monument. A little ways beyond at 57.4 it drops down through a rocky SSS area, where there is actually a bluffline, sort of. You don't see too many real bluffs in the Ouachitas like you do in the Ozarks.

There are several rock gardens, and a few large pines as the trail continues on mostly level. It rises up a little more and comes to an intersection with a road trace at 57.8. (look for Black Mtn. Shelter at 57.8) The white-blazed Black Fork Mountain Wilderness Trail continues up the hill to the left, and the OT TURNS RIGHT and heads down the hill. (The Black Fork Mountain Trail is detailed in my **Arkansas Hiking Trails** guidebook. It is a great hike up there, and I highly recommend it as a separate hike. Some folks make the trip up and back down again in the same day, but I prefer to carry my backpack and spend the night.)

The hike downhill is pretty nice, and soon the road levels out and eases to the right, past MILEPOST #58. Just beyond this, as you come to an open, congested area, the trail leaves the roadbed TO THE LEFT, and heads out into the level woods as just trail. It soon drops on down the hill and intersects with another road trace—TURN LEFT and follow the trace downhill. It eventually swings on around to the right, intersects with another road trace in the bottom—TURN RIGHT—and runs on out to and across FR #516 at 58.5. This is Eagle Gap. (This road goes out to the right to Hwy. 270.)

From the road the trail comes to and crosses Clear Fork, which is about the only reliable water supply for a long, long ways along the trail—until nearly the end of this section at 67.7. Be sure to fill up. It is usually a dry crossing.

From there the trail heads upstream, rising slightly, on good trail. It rises up away from the creek, crosses a couple of dry drains, past MILEPOST #59. There is a wizard tree or two around. I would like to say again that the trail through here is in great shape. The heavier your backpack is, the more you appreciate good trail.

The trail joins an old road trace for a short distance, goes through a rock field and heads up into a ravine. It crosses the ravine and swings back to the right on the opposite hillside. It levels off somewhat and begins to wander around near the top of the ridge. All of this hill from Clear Fork on for a long ways is actually part of Fourche Mountain. In fact I guess we are on it almost all the way to Big Brushy Campground—over thirty miles. Good grief, that's a long mountain!

My tape recorder said "decent trail, nice open woods, big pines, pleasant walk." What more could you ask for? The trail rises up a little, makes one sharp turn to the right, then eases down a little. At 59.7 all of a sudden there are a number of rock piles, which make for an SSS. And then they're gone.

The trail joins a road trace and heads uphill some, and comes to a "T" intersection—TURN LEFT and continue to follow the road trace up the hill. Just beyond is MILEPOST #60. The road trace soon levels off on the ridgetop, then drops down the hill past a wildlife pond (full of frogs) on the right at 60.2.

It eases uphill some more, then just as the road begins to steepen, the trail leaves it TO THE LEFT and continues as plain trail. We will do this a *lot* during the next several miles. In fact, there is a pattern that you will soon notice: The trail will generally follow the ridgeline, sometimes as plain trail, often on an old road. Then, as it approaches a knoll or steeper section of the ridge, it will veer to one side or the other. And it weaves through a lot of saddles in much the same way. There are still a lot of ups and downs on this section, but the trail will miss a lot of the steeper ones that are possible.

It continues up the hill a little, and there is a leaf-off SSS view through the trees back behind and to the left of the end of Black Fork Mountain, and the tower on Rich Mountain. The trail levels out some as it swings on around the hillside, but there are a few steeper, rocky spots. There is an SSS area of big boulders and wizards at 60.9. The trail goes level through a saddle in the ridge (what did I tell ya), and begins to run along the right side of it, past MILEPOST #61.

The trail crosses a steep, rocky hillside, rising up here and there, through several small drainages, but not too bad. We will be crossing many, many of these smaller drainages. Some of them have running water in them during the wet periods, but most would be dry the rest of the time.

At 61.2 the trail passes a giant, three-pronged dogwood tree. It's a huckleberry hillside up above, and a rock garden one below. The trail swings up to the left, past more wizards and big pines, and a small drain, and heads up to and through another saddle at 61.7. Like many of the zillions of saddles that we're going to be going through, there is a great campsite location in this one.

The trail continues along level for a while, across a rocky hillside, then dips down a bit through a drain or two, past MILEPOST #62. There are lots and lots of rocks through here, and the trail is well-dug into some of them. It rises up to an SSS at 62.2, where there is a large oak that leans out over one of the rock fields. And there is a nice view there too. The trail levels out just beyond, then crosses a couple of those smaller drains, and rises up some to and through another saddle at 62.3. Many times the trail is lined with rocks (intentionally) on both sides as it goes through these saddles. Nice touch. Good campsite here.

Through the saddle the trail eases up to the left a little, across a rocky hillside. Then it eases back downhill some, past a wizard or two, into a section of real thick underbrush. Quickly the woods open up again, and the trail rises up to and climbs up through a narrow, rocky ridgeline at 62.9, an SSS. This is a genuine "razorback" ridge. The trail turns to the right and follows this hogback, easing uphill some, past MILEPOST #63.

Right in the area of the MILEPOST is a terrific SSS view. You can see not only Black Fork and Rich Mountains, but also the Lodge at Queen Wilhelmina, and even the microwave tower that we passed back at mile 48.4. Nice view. There are lots of pretty good views out from these ridgetops as we hike along, especially during leaf-off. Usually what you are looking at are the other ridges around, some of them you've already been on, others you're heading to. I highly recommend that you hike during leaf-off.

From there the trail continues uphill along a smoother ridgetop now. Then soon goes through the rocks again, into a real dense underbrush area. It swings back and forth across the ridge several times. At 63.3 there is an SSS area where the ridge rocks extend for a ways and are moss-covered. There are several big wizards standing guard too. Past the end of it the trail swings to the right, then straight *up* into another rock pile. At the first landing there is a nice SSS view.

The trail climbs up the rocky ridge some more, through lots of scrub trees. It does some up-and-downing near the ridgetop, then levels through a saddle at 63.9. The hillside has gone up on our right now, and we're heading around the left side of the ridge, past MILEPOST #64. Lots of wizard trees on the steep hillside. And even a few big oaks. The trail gets rocky in places. It crosses several narrow rocky slide areas and seeps. Some of the rock slides have water running down inside them. I guess these slides are old rock glaciers, that have pretty much stopped moving, and have moss and heavy lichens growing on them. Does this mean that the old saying about a rolling stone gathers no moss is true?

There are some good leaf-off views through here up to the north, and to the ridges in the distance. The trail levels off and passes through a saddle at 64.5, then heads down the other side of the ridge to the right. This begins one of the most expansive boulder fields that

I've ever seen in Arkansas. And it's kind of weird because although the boulders seem to extend out forever, there is a normal forest growing up right out of them. And there are lots of big wizards taking care of the place. A definite SSS, all of it. And even the trail is pretty neat. This is probably the first man-made SSS—the trail is dug so deep into the rocks, it's just amazing. I'm sure glad that I wasn't around to work on this trail crew!

The trail continues winding on down the hill through the boulders. In some stretches the rocks have fallen back down onto the trail, and the footing is miserable. So watch your step. Especially right after leaf fall. At times the trail is waist deep in the rocks. Like at 64.7, another wonderful part of the SSS. Then there is a short stretch where there is no trail at all—follow the blazes.

It leaves the rock gardens and drops on down to a saddle, and runs along the ridgetop. Just as the ridge begins to rise up, we pass MILEPOST #65. The trail veers off to the left, and rises some, across another rocky hillside. Many of these ridges that the trail skirts around the high sections of have rocky tops. If you've got the energy and the time, some of them may be worth exploring, and probably have good views. You can see them much better during leaf-off.

The trail continues through more rock gardens, then drops on down some to another saddle at 65.3. It runs up the middle of the ridge, then swings to the left side of the hill and continues to rise. There are some thick briar patches through here. It quickly levels across a steep hillside. Some of the trail is a little rocky too. It drops on down some, swings to the right, and passes through some nasty trail for a short stretch—bad footing. It runs level between the boulder fields some. My recorder said "...pretty good trail through some sections, no trail in others. A hillside of rock..."

MILEPOST #66 is just before a huge "N" oak tree up on the right. The trail grade is mostly moderate through here. But it begins to drop a little more, past a minor SSS area at 66.3. There is a small spring there, and the rocks are covered with thick moss. I wonder if a moss coat would be warm?

During leaf-off you can see a pretty good mountain out in front and off in the distance—this is the continuation of Fourche Mountain on the other side of Hwy. 71. We will be climbing up there in a little while. It looks pretty big. You can also see Foran Gap, the low spot where the trail crosses Hwy. 71. And speaking of Hwy. 71, you may get a glimpse of it down off in the valley to the left in this area.

The trail does some up-and-downing, and crosses a dry drain or two. It swings to the right around the hillside at 66.7 and enters a wonderful pine forest oasis—there are *no* rocks. A neat little SSS. It doesn't last for long though, as the trail re-enters a rocky area and levels off. It swings to the left across several dry drains, does some up-and-downing through the rocks, then passes MILEPOST #67 as it eases down the hill. Lots and lots of huckleberry in this area. And in May there are many blooming wild azalea bushes. You'll see these along many other parts of the trail as well. You can look around on the ground and find some of those neat reindeer lichens too. These are the light-colored, weird looking, thick lichens (others call them mosses) that are hard and brittle in the winter, but soft the rest of the year.

The trail continues to drop on down the hill, and passes an SSS at 67.2. There is a waterfall just up on the right. This falls can really get cooking during periods of heavy rain. The trail eases down some more, winding on around the hillside. It works its way to the right into a draw, and crosses a stream at 67.7 (the largest that we've seen since Clark Fork back at 58.5). Of course this is an SSS. There are a couple of waterfalls, and even, oh my gosh, a tiny swimming hole! I would say that there is water here in all but the driest of times. This is the *last* water that you are likely to see for quite some time. The next reliable water is at Tan-A-Hill Spring, mile 74.2.

The trail swings to the left, rises up just a tad, then levels and begins a leisurely stroll towards Hwy. 71. This is a wonderful little hike—an SSS forest walk. It passes MILEPOST #68, then comes out to a makeshift parking area and Hwy. 71 at 68.1. This is Foran Gap, and the end of Section Three. By the way, this last little stretch of trail makes a great little short hike up to the pool area from the highway.

SECTION FOUR—26.4 miles
Hwy. 71 to Big Brushy Campground (Hwy. 270)

Trail Point	Mile Point	Mileage West to East	Mileage East to West
Foran Gap/Hwy. 71	68.1	0.0	26.4
Foran Gap Shelter	68.9	.8	25.6
Tan-A-Hill Gap	74.1	6.0	20.4
Turner Creek Gap Shelter	79.9	11.8	14.6
FR #76A	85.5	17.4	9.1
FR #76	86.0	17.9	8.5
FR #48	88.2	20.1	6.3
FR #813	90.3	22.2	4.2
Brushy Creek Mtn. Shelter	90.6	22.5	3.9
Brushy Creek Trail	91.4	23.3	3.1
FR #6	94.3	26.2	.2
Big Brushy C. G.	94.5	26.4	0.0

Section Four begins at the Hwy. 71/Foran Gap Trailhead, about six miles north of Acorn. The first part of this section (to mile 85.0) is located on the Poteau Ranger District (office in Waldron), and the rest of it is on the Oden Ranger District (office in Oden), all in the Ouachita National Forest. Quads are Acorn, Y City, Buck Knob, and Brushy Creek Mtn.

This is a *long, high and dry* section, so be sure that you carry plenty of water. In fact, **you may not find any reliable water during real dry seasons anywhere on the entire section!** Please re-read the last sentence. Your best bet for water along the way is Tan-A-Hill Spring, which is 6.1 miles in at 74.2 (spur trail detour). It is also a good idea to stash water at FR #48 where it intersects with FR #76, which is 20.1 miles in at mile 88.2 (or even at the crossing of FR #76 at 86.0).

Most of this section is pretty easy hiking, but there is one very tough climb, and, of course, lots of other lesser ones. The trail is up on Fourche Mountain for what seems like forever, runs along a forest road for a while, then crosses a couple of other mountains before dropping down to the end at Big Brushy Campground. Views everywhere.

The trail crosses Hwy. 71 at mile 68.1 and heads up an old road to the left (now closed). Sign in at the registration box. The trail will be on this road trace for several miles. It rises on up the hill and curves around to the right, levels off some, then continues to rise up to 68.8. There is a lesser road to the right here—stay on the main road trace straight ahead. (look for Foran Gap Shelter at 68.9) MILEPOST #69 is just beyond.

You are now on the ridge top of Fourche Mountain, which the trail has actually been running along ever since Eagle Gap at mile 58.5. Most of this section is basically on this same mountain, all the way to

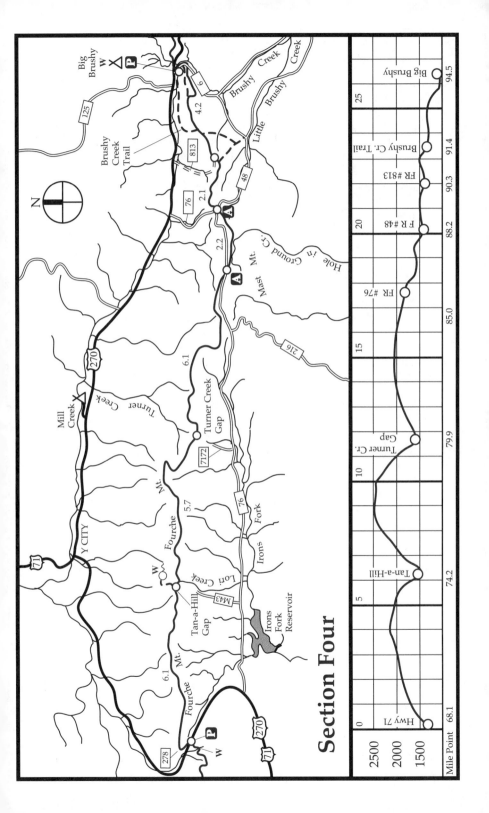

Section Four

89.0. The trail remains on this ridge for quite a while. It does rise up a little more, past some good campsites, dips through a saddle, and continues along on the old road trace, getting more grown up as you go—nice walking.

There are a few good views to the south as the trail continues to rise up a little on the right side of the ridge, past MILEPOST #70. During leaf-off you can see more of the Ouachita Mountains in the distance. At 70.4 the trail has leveled somewhat and there is an SSS rock formation just above it on the left. All of this area is pretty easy hiking, even the uphill parts. It is level as it passes MILEPOST #71.

The trail curves back and forth a little, and does some up-and-downing, going through a saddle at 71.3, then heads uphill some. At 71.7 there is a wildlife pond on the right, which was dry when I came through. You can really appreciate the road bed as it heads down through a boulder field—there are no rocks in the road. It heads down the hill, through a saddle, then back uphill again, past MILEPOST #72.

The road curves right and left, then in the middle of a long stretch uphill at 72.1 the trail leaves the road TO THE RIGHT. Be sure to watch for this. The old trail stayed on the road, climbing up to a fire tower on top of Wolf Pinnacle, then back down the other side (only the footings of the tower remain). This new section of trail stays mostly level and goes around it. If you do happen to miss this turn, just stay on the road and you will eventually intersect the trail again, but you'll be breathing hard.

This section is plain, wide trail that runs mostly level across a rocky hillside, past a couple of dry drains. It swings to the right, then left across a flat, and back into the steep hillside again. Lots of huckleberry. There is an SSS rock formation at 72.7. Soon the terrain levels out and we intersect with the old road trace again at 72.8—TURN RIGHT and continue along the middle of the ridgetop. There isn't really much of a road here now—most of the ridgetop roads that we will follow for a while will be nothing more than faint traces, like this one.

The trail climbs up some, then veers to the right side of the ridge (trail reroute for a little while), and eases on down the hill past MILEPOST #73. It continues to drop but soon levels and smooths out through a saddle. Like the trail on the west side of Hwy. 71, we will be going through lots of saddles, and there will be good campsites at most of them. Of course, water is always a problem, but during the wet season you could probably head off of either side and eventually find some.

Beyond the saddle the trail heads uphill at a pretty good clip, passes a minor SSS rock outcrop, and there is a good leaf-off view back behind us. You may notice a heavy wire beside the trail here, and off and on for the next few miles. This wire used to be a telephone link that led up to the fire lookout tower on Wolf Pinnacle. It was used to report fires.

The trail soon levels out and begins to head back down the hill to another saddle, still mostly along the middle of the ridgetop. It is kind of rocky in spots. It levels through the saddle, dropping some more. It passes MILEPOST #74, then drops on down the hill and passes through Tan-A-Hill Gap at 74.1, and there are some great campsites here.

Go across the four-wheeler road and begin to head uphill on an old historical wagon road, this was the first highway through the area. The trail only follows it for a short distance. As the hill gets steeper, at 74.2, the trail leaves the road TO THE RIGHT.

There is a spring near here. To get to it, *stay* on the old wagon road instead of turning off of it. The Tan-A-Hill Spring is .3 mile up the road and around the corner, on the right. You will see lots of tall ferns growing around it (may or may not have water). This was the water source for a family that lived nearby. Like many of the springs high in the hills these days, this one can dry up when you least expect it to, and you may not be able to count on it as a reliable water supply all year long. When you do find water here, this may be the *last* water that you will see until Big Brushy Campground at 94.5, so *fill up* if you can.

Now back to the trail. It leaves the wagon road to the right, and heads into the woods on the level. There are several huge pine trees scattered through this area. The trail crosses a dry drain as it runs around the right side of the rocky hill, then begins to drop. It gets a little steep, and rocky. During leaf-off there is a pretty good view out ahead, and down into the ravines that we're obviously headed into.

The trail used to drop down into a pretty little creek named Lori Creek, but it no longer does so. It was a really steep climb up out of that ravine, which the trail now completely bypasses. Pretty good water source though.

The trail continues to run along the top of a ridge and levels out some through a saddle. Then it takes off on the right side of the ridge and continues to climb through a boulder field, but not near as steep. You can see Irons Fork Lake off to the right in the distance through the trees. The trail levels some, then heads back uphill kind of steep past MILEPOST #75. The telephone wire is around again. In fact there is even one of those white insulators here. The trail finally levels again as it goes through a saddle in the ridge. There are lots of lichen-covered rocks along the way, but the trail is smooth.

The hillside is steep and rocky as the trail makes its away around the right side of the hill, staying mostly level. There is an "N" tree here and there, which we haven't seen too many of lately. The trail eventually heads up the hill at a pretty good clip, through an SSS of slab rock at 75.5. There is a great view out to the right, and a bunch of stunted trees. The trail levels out as the briars get really grown up. There are tons of spring wildflowers growing up through the briars.

The trail runs along the left side of the ridge, which it hasn't done for a while, drops down, then back up again. There are a few wizard trees hanging around. It eases across the ridge, past lots of lichen rocks, then runs along the right side of the ridge, mostly level. It rises some, back on the middle of the ridge, then tops out and passes MILEPOST #76. It runs level for a while, veers to the left side, then to the right, and begins to drop on down pretty steep. Good view.

It levels through a saddle, then heads up again, through more thick briars. Profuse wildflowers all around. The trail swings to the right side of the ridge a little, then back to the middle, heading uphill some. At 76.5 there is an SSS up on the left—a bluff rock ridge with a stunted pine tree growing right out of it. The trail gets nearly completely covered with briars. Hope you're not wearing shorts! Near the end of the rock ridge the trail heads uphill to a saddle. Good campsites. Then it continues up some more to an SSS view just beyond—a great view of the Ouachitas.

The trail heads up the ridge some more, through lots of briars. It runs along the right side of the ridge, climbing at a pretty good clip. Just where it levels off for a moment is MILEPOST #77. It continues swinging uphill, now around the left side of the ridge. Then it rejoins the middle of the ridge and begins to head downhill at a pretty good clip. It swings to the left and gets pretty steep, and finally levels back on the middle of the ridge. It heads downhill some more, going through a beautiful wide saddle at 77.6.

From the saddle the trail eases around the right side of the ridge, then heads uphill steeply, through lots of briars. There is a pretty good view out over the scrub brush. It's real thick. At one point the trail climbs up over a rock embankment, then back into the thick brush. It levels and quickly begins to drop down the middle of the ridge. (Am I beginning to sound like a broken record yet?) And as always, the next hilltop comes into view out in front. I really like hiking during leaf-off—you can just see so much more around you.

The trail levels off and goes through a long saddle. MILEPOST #78 is at the far end, just before the trail heads downhill again. It drops along the right side of another saddle, past a tiny stream (it was just a trickle, but I got water in this drainage when I was here—I wouldn't count on it though), and continues down the hill on the right side of the ridge. It gets rocky in a spot or two, and the trail levels through a hillside of scrub brush. There's a nice open SSS view there at 78.2.

From the great view, the trail heads down the hill at a pretty good clip, then levels off and runs on the left side of the ridge. There are lots of big oaks in this area. And rocks too. It crosses the ridge again and heads back downhill on the right, then level, then back on over to the ridge. Another nice view out ahead through the trees—an SSS during leaf-off. The trail drops a little, passes through another saddle, and just as it begins to head uphill it passes MILEPOST #79.

It stays on the ridgetop, easing up some, then runs level. There are a few wizards around, and some rocks. It goes through a saddle at 79.5, and eases up the ridge, then levels. Great campsites. Before long the trail goes right off the end of the ridge, and heads steeply down the hill. It swings to the right as the grade lessons up some, but still heading down. (look for Turner Gap Shelter at 79.9) It levels in a saddle at 79.9 and crosses a four-wheeler road. The topo map shows a different Turner Creek on each side of the mountain here, so we'll call this spot Turner Creek Gap.

From there it heads back uphill again, past MILEPOST #80. Just beyond, the trail lands on the ridgetop, turns left and continues uphill some along it. The ridge gets a little wider and steeper. Lots of big oaks. The trail swings to the left side of it, and the grade gets less steep.

This is a nice, wide open stretch of woods. We ease up to the right some, then left, then along the right side of the ridge. The hillside gets pretty steep and rocky. The trail swings to the left on around the nose of the ridge, then drops down to a saddle. The trail runs level through the saddle, and at the other end, just as the ridge begins to rise a little, is MILEPOST #81.

From there the trail heads around the right side of the rocky ridge, rising a little, but mostly level. It passes through another saddle at 81.4 and runs along the left side of the ridge. It crosses a tiny drain, then runs level to another saddle and past a couple of big cedar trees. It continues to run mostly level, dropping just a little, through another saddle. Plenty of good campsites. Towards the end of the saddle the trail heads around the right side, as the rocky ridge rises up to the left. There are some nice rock formations up on the ridge.

The trail is mostly level, then rises up just a little to rejoin the ridge. It turns right and runs along it past MILEPOST #82. It stays on the ridgetop, easing down through another saddle, then up some, then through another saddle. It eases up some more, past a nice SSS rock outcrop up on the right at 82.4. Then it drops some down to and through another saddle. From there the trail rises up through the rocks around the right side of the ridge. It rejoins the ridgetop and heads on down to another saddle, passing MILEPOST #83 along the way. There are lots of huckleberry bushes through here.

The trail heads back uphill, and intersects with an old road trace on top—TURN RIGHT and follow the road (be alert to this if hiking west). It soon begins to head downhill on the left side of the ridge, levels out through a couple of different saddles, then rises back uphill again. It quickly levels, then drops to another saddle at 83.8. The trail leaves this old road TO THE LEFT here, and continues along through the saddle on the level.

Soon the trail begins to head up the ridge, and it gets pretty steep. Near the top is MILEPOST #84. The trail levels out a little ways beyond, and generally follows the ridgetop. There are lots of briars through here, some large oaks and pines, and a few good views through the trees. The trail rises up a little, past lichen-covered rocks, and good footing. It swings to the right some, dropping on down the hill, and comes alongside FR #76.

The trail runs level across the hillside, rising past MILEPOST #85. It levels off a bit and then veers to the left away from the forest road, and climbs up just a bit around a small ridge to the right. (We have now left the Poteau Ranger District and are in the Oden Ranger District. We will be in this District all the way to Hwy. 27 at 121.7. The next three miles of trail is a reroute done in 2011 with the wide trail machine—the old route used to be on the forest road all that distance.)

The trail levels out near the forest road again, then crosses FR #76A at 85.5. The trail sticks near the main forest road, dropping and weaving a bit, then drops a little, passes MILEPOST #86, and comes out to and across FR #76, an access point with space for a couple of cars.

The trail crosses FR #76 and curves to the left through some nice rock formations. We'll be on the south side of a long ridge for a couple of miles, with some good leaf-off views to the south.

The trail drops down through a saddle and then into a drainage that is off to the right where the trail becomes an old road trace. It drops down a bit more, levels out past MILEPOST #87, then rises up a bit and passes through another saddle. The trail leaves the road bed and veers to the left (wide machine trail again), up and around a hill, then runs level a bit, then curves around to the left and down, then back to the right. The trail finally cuts back down to the left and though a saddle next to FR #76—we get back onto normal trail here at 87.7 (end of the big reroute).

The trail heads up into a beautiful pine forest, lots of huckleberry, and the trail is soft underfoot (roads are usually hard on the feet). It swings away from the road, levels off, then works its way around a small ridge. It drops on down the hill, comes alongside the forest road, and passes MILEPOST #88. From there it drops down a little more, past several huge pine trees, across FR #48 at 88.2, which intersects with FR #76 at this same point. It's about 2 miles from here to Hwy. 270 via FR #76. This is a good spot on this section to stash some water, and it's easy to get to from the highway (turnoff is 11.7 miles east of Y-City, 4.7 miles west of Big Brushy Campground).

Across the road, the trail eases up through a stand of pines, past a registration box, through a rocky area, curves to the right, and crosses a drainage. If you are out of water and desperate, I would follow this drainage downhill until you find water. It might be a ways. The trail runs level along the left side of a hill, then rises slightly, working around the right-hand side of the hill. Lots and lots of huckleberry, and a few giant pines.

It runs level across the hillside for a while, then eases up past MILEPOST #89. There is an SSS just beyond—several large squared-off boulders are next to the trail. From there it crosses a ridge of sorts, a divide that apparently signifies a transition from the Fourche Mountain Range to some lesser ones.

We are hiking along the side of Rockhouse Mountain right now. The mountain that can be seen out ahead as the trail heads downhill some is Brushy Creek Mountain, which we will soon be hiking along, and will in fact follow all the way to Big Brushy Campground. (Technically, this is all still probably the Fourche Mountains, but I could not find it labeled as such on any maps.)

The trail continues to make its way on around the hill and down to an SSS view at 89.6. The trail levels somewhat as the ridge comes down from the right. There are scattered rock outcrops here and there, and a couple of small drainages. The trail passes MILEPOST #90, then swings to the left and heads on down the hill. Just beyond the trail hits an old road trace—TURN RIGHT and follow this road.

It leads down into a saddle between the two mountains. There is a lesser road at 90.2 that goes on over to the right to a wildlife pond (stay on the main road). Just beyond, the road levels out and comes to a trail intersection. The Rockhouse Trail goes to the right 1.8 miles, and is blazed with white paint. (This little trail is part of the Brushy Trail Complex, and eventually comes out onto FR #6, which we are going to come out on also.)

The OT continues STRAIGHT AHEAD, and immediately crosses FR #813 at 90.3. You can access this spot from Hwy. 270, which is a couple miles to the left, but I hear the road is pretty rough—I wouldn't try it with a car.

The trail heads up the hill a little—this is now Brushy Creek Mountain, our home to the end of this section. It does some up-and-downing and crosses a couple of little rocky drains. (look for Brushy Creek Shelter at 90.6) At 90.6 a road trace comes up from the right and joins the trail (continue straight ahead), and runs steeply up a hill. At 90.8 the trail leaves the road TO THE LEFT, and heads up into the woods as just plain trail. There were lots of violets popping out all over when I came through in March.

It continues across the hillside, around the nose of a ridge to the left. It levels out up on top and runs along the ridgetop, past MILEPOST #91. It eases along the ridge, then swings to the left and begins to drop across the steep, rocky hillside. There is an unusual "N" tree (aren't they all) on the right. At 91.4 the trail levels off in a saddle and comes to a couple of different trail intersections—CONTINUE STRAIGHT AHEAD.

(The first trail goes to the right and is the Mountain Top Trail. This short trail heads back about a mile to the right, over a rocky ridge, and ends at a forest road. And the second trail, just a few feet beyond, is the Brushy Creek Trail. It heads down the hill to the left and makes its way 3.6 miles to Big Brushy Campground. This trail, when combined with the rest of this section of the OT ahead, makes a nice 6.9-mile loop from the campground. A map and complete description of this loop is shown in my *Arkansas Hiking Trails* guidebook. Both of these side trails are blazed white.)

The main trail eases up the ridge some, then follows the ridge downhill at a pretty good clip, and finally levels off, passing MILE-POST #92. There is a nice SSS rock outcrop off to the right just beyond. The trail drops down some, through a saddle, then heads back uphill again. (There is an off-trail SSS rock formation off to the left through the woods—a pretty nice view too.) The trail goes around the right side of the hill, then heads on down to another saddle at 92.5. Just as it heads up the hill again, there is an intersection with the Brushy Mountain Trail. This trail goes to the left on down the hill to FR #6 and Big Brushy Campground, creating a 3.5 mile loop, and is blazed white. The OT continues STRAIGHT AHEAD at this intersection, and heads up the hill.

It again goes around the right side of the ridge, across a dry drain, to an SSS rocky ridge up above the trail to the left at 92.9. There are some good leaf-off views too. From there it swings up the hill to the left, kind of doubling back, up and over the ridgetop, then heads down the other side past MILEPOST #93. There are several SSS views here through the trees—you can see lots and lots of ridges off in the distance, and Brushy Creek down below.

The trail does some up-and-downing, down through blackjack oaks, and lots of wildflowers. It runs level some, but generally makes its way down the hillside, and crosses a number of tiny dry drains. Lots of big pines and a few large oaks too. It passes MILEPOST #94 on the way down. Just beyond, the trail turns to the right some and follows down the middle of a side ridge, over to the corner of a cut area, which is growing up rapidly with a herd of little pines. The trail picks up an old road trace there, and follows it down the hill, back into regular woods. At 94.2, just as the road gets ready to head down a steep hill, the trail leaves the road TO THE LEFT, and continues down the hill through the woods as plain trail.

It drops quickly down to FR #6 at 94.3—TURN LEFT and follow this road. It runs alongside Big Brushy Creek that we saw a glimpse of from up on the ridge. A little ways beyond, just before the road crosses Brushy Creek on a large bridge, the Brushy Mountain Trail takes off up the hill to the left at a nice wood landing. This is the trail that intersects with the OT back up on the hill, and makes a nice loop through this area.

The OT continues across the road—Big Brushy Campground and Hwy. 270 are just across the other side. There is a trailhead parking area there, with campsites and a picnic shelter, but there may not be any drinking water—use the creek. The turnoff road that goes into the campground is at 94.5. This is the end of Section Four.

SECTION FIVE—27.2 miles
Big Brushy Campground (Hwy. 270) to Hwy. 27

Trail Point	Mile Point	Mileage West to East	Mileage East to West
Big Brushy Camp	94.5	0.0	27.2
FR #33	96.0	1.5	25.7
Blowout Mountain	96.8	2.3	24.9
Fiddler Creek Shelter	100.9	6.4	20.8
FR #274 West cross	101.0	6.5	20.7
Fiddlers Creek	101.1	6.6	20.6
FR #274 East cross	102.0	7.5	19.7
FR #149	105.5	11.0	16.2
Rainy Creek	105.6	11.1	16.1
Suck Mountain Shelter	108.6	14.1	13.1
Suck Mountain	108.7	14.2	13.0
Round Top Trail	114.1	19.6	7.6
Story Creek Shelter (Chalybeate Spring)	116.7	22.2	5.0
Womble Trail	117.2	22.7	4.5
FR #149/Muddy Cr.	118.7	24.2	3.0
Smith Creek	121.1	26.6	.6
Hwy. 27 Trailhead	121.7	27.2	0.0

Section Five begins at Big Brushy Campground, which is located on Hwy. 270 between Y-City and Pencil Bluff. All of this section is on the Oden Ranger District, and their office is located just outside of Oden on Hwy. 88. Quads are Brushy Creek Mountain, Sims, Story, Chula Mountain and Onyx (the trail just barely touches the last two maps).

The water situation on this section is much better. The trail route follows several mountains, but drops down and crosses nice streams in between. Even a spot or two to take a dip! There are a couple of pretty serious climbs in this section, though perhaps not as bad as some we have seen. There is still lots of up-and-downing, but the grades and the hills seem to be getting a little smaller. There are a number of access points, so you can hike short stretches if you want to.

The campground is right on Big Brushy Creek, but it doesn't get used very much. It is next to the highway, and gets a little noisy when the traffic is heavy, which doesn't happen too often. There is a trail system all its own here. At least six hiking trails can be accessed from the campground, and two or more of them combine with the Ouachita Trail (west of the campground) to form nice loops. The Brushy Creek Trail is detailed in my *Arkansas Hiking Trails* guidebook. Be sure to check with the District office in Oden for current information—they are really doing a great job of expanding the trail system here.

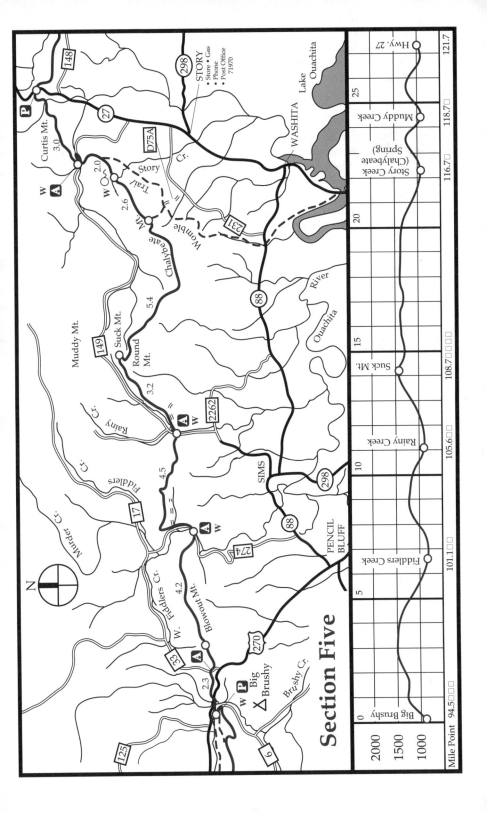

Section Five

There is a trailhead parking area here, campsites and a picnic shelter, but there may not be any drinking water—you can always use the creek.

 The trail description of this section begins right at the turnoff into the campground, on FR #6, which is at OT mile point 94.5. From there the trail follows the forest road out towards Hwy. 270, then leaves the road TO THE RIGHT just before the highway. It heads across a flat as plain trail.

A sign here says that the Oden Woods and Water Club maintains the next part of the trail. This is a great idea—if you are interested, check with the District office about adopting a section of your own. The trail swings away from the highway and comes alongside Big Brushy Creek. There are some nice, big trees in here. It quickly heads back to the highway and crosses a swampy area. From here you need to get up on the shoulder of the road and cross a creek while on the highway. Right at the end of the bridge, leave the highway TO THE LEFT and head on up into the woods.

As the trail climbs on up the hill it passes MILEPOST #95. It continues to climb up some, heading on around the left side of a ridge. It levels off some here and there, just rising slightly. There are a couple of spots here where you might see several pine trees cut down along the trail. These are trees that got infested with destructive bugs and had to be cut down. The trail finally levels off near the top of the ridge, then begins to drop slightly, and comes to FR #33.

The trail crosses this road at an angle to the right, crosses a dry drain, and comes to MILEPOST #96. It winds on around the side of the ridge, rising a little, next to the forest road. It swings to the left past a couple of dry drains and a wildlife pond at 96.3, then turns into the hill and climbs a little steeper.

Just as the trail hits the top of the ridge (but not the top of the hill), it meets an old fence line, turns to the left and heads steeply *up* the ridge. We will be seeing a lot of this fence in this section. It used to mark the boundary of the old Muddy Creek Wildlife Management Area. Most of the signs on the posts saying this have faded. The climb up is steep and rocky. By the way, this is Blowout Mountain, and we will be on it for a while. I could never get the same answer twice when I quizzed folks about how it got that name, so I guess you can make up your own. This area is also marked on some maps as the Blowout Mountain Scenic Area.

The steep, rocky climb continues. There are a lot of wild plum and service berry trees through here, which were in full bloom in March. There are some spotty views back behind as you head up. The trail eventually levels off at 96.8, past some nice rock outcrops below the trail, and eases on down a little. It levels off along the left side of the ridge, past MILEPOST #97. The fence line pretty much goes down the middle of the ridge, and the trail follows it here and there.

There are some good views out through the trees to the north once in a while. And there is a long stretch of briars, which could get bad in the summer. The tread gets a little rocky, so watch your step. Soon the trail swings to the left, past a nice big boulder, and switchbacks down the steep hillside. It passes thorough a rock garden area where the trail has been dug out a couple of feet deep. Haven't we been here before? You can tell that a great deal of hard work went into building this trail. The rocks are nice, but watch your footing.

It does some up-and-downing, across a steep, rocky hillside, and through a large rock garden SSS area at 97.7. There isn't much of a trail tread through it though. The trail crosses many more of these rock gardens, mostly on the level. It is dug out well through some of them, and not at all in others. At one of them it looks like the crew started to dig out a nice patch, then got tired and quit. The trail passes MILEPOST #98 while on the level.

It passes a couple more rock gardens, rises up just a little, then levels off again, and passes several "N" trees. The view out is a little different here and there. Unfortunately, most of the views through here overlook clear-cuts. Oh well, if we didn't grow trees for lumber and paper here, there would not be a National Forest, and, of course, no trail. It is up to us (Joe Q. Public) to see to it that the Forest Service manages these lands for multiple use (which includes hiking *and* timber harvesting). All in all it is hard to love a clear-cut though.

It does some more up-and-downing across the steep, rocky hillside, crosses a ditch, then eases on up the hill to MILEPOST #99. Soon beyond the trail joins the ridge and heads downhill on it, swinging to the left side and back again a couple of times. It begins to lose altitude rapidly, levels briefly at 99.6, passing through a saddle at 99.7, then heads around to the right side of the ridge for the first time.

The trail eases up the hill on the right side some, then levels off through thick underbrush and a few more rocks. It swings to the left and uphill right at a giant SSS pine tree. MILEPOST #100 is also at that spot. This is a neat spot. I believe the trail was built right here just so we could enjoy this wonderful tree, which is a fitting salute to the 100th mile of the Ouachita Trail.

From there the trail heads uphill, up through the rocks, then soon comes to the ridgetop and levels off. It winds around some, past reindeer lichens covering the forest floor, and one of the wildlife management signs that has acted as a registration station. It eases to the left a little and begins a downhill run, past a big pile of rocks at 100.5 up on the ridge. It goes through a saddle on the right, and continues down the hill. (look for Fiddler Creek Shelter at 100.9) At 100.9 the trail crosses an old log road trace, joins a branch of it and heads steeply down the hill.

Just as the trail levels there is a terrific SSS rock outcrop up on the left—this is perhaps the biggest chunk of rock that we've seen on the trail. A really neat spot worth exploring (just don't fall off). The trail leaves the log road to the right just after this and intersects with FR #274—TURN LEFT and follow the road. MILEPOST #101 is right here. Fiddlers Creek is just across the road, and it is an SSS as well. There is a great swimming hole there. Not bad campsites either, if you don't mind being near the road. Water all year.

The trail will be on this road for about a mile. It crosses the creek at 101.1 (Beautiful water—time for lunch!), then rises up just a little and swings away from the creek, and levels. It passes a huge field off on the left at 101.6. There is a giant, curvy pine tree here next to the road. And soon after you can look up ahead and see the spine of Rock Row Mountain, which we will be climbing up the back side of in a little while. It is just as the name says, a row of rocks.

It crosses a side stream (which could be a wet crossing during high water) at 101.8. Be sure to fill your jugs. On the other side a lesser forest road, #E02 takes off to the right—stay on the main road. We pass below the end of that rocky ridge that we saw, and just beyond the trail leaves the forest road TO THE RIGHT, and heads up into the woods, past MILEPOST #102.

There is good trail here as it heads up the mountain, first around the left side, then swinging back to the right some. The hillside is very steep, and covered with huckleberry and reindeer. The trail gets pretty steep too. We are working our way up the backside of that Rock Row ridgetop that we saw from the road, although we can't really see it. The grade finally gets a little less, levels for a moment, then heads uphill some more. There is one spot where you could drop your pack and wander over to the right side of the ridgetop for a view.

It continues up the left side of the ridge, then level some past a cedar tree, then some up-and-downing near the top of the ridge. During leaf-off you can look out ahead and see the ridges beyond. Soon the trail heads on down the hill a little more, past a turkey, and MILE-POST #103. From there it heads much steeper down the hill, swinging back and forth. It levels off on the ridge at 103.2 (great campsites), then resumes downhill. It switchbacks on down through a level spot, and crosses a small creek (another great campsite) at 103.3, then heads up-hill, back to the right.

It switchbacks up, past more huckleberry and reindeer, lands on a ridge and continues heading up, and at a pretty good clip. It swings to the right, and levels through a saddle at 103.6, turns right, then left past a rock formation, and begins to drop a little. There are several lines of rock outcrops in this area. They add a nice touch. At one point the trail swings right up into and through one hogback of rock. It heads off the end of the rock pile and continues along the middle of the ridge, mostly on the level.

Just as the trail starts up the hill it passes MILEPOST #104, then curves around the right side of a hill and runs level some. It passes through a saddle at 104.3. There is a deep ravine off to the left, and lots of huckleberry all around. It eases around the left side of the ridge now, heading downhill, some level, lots of reindeer. It runs level for a while, through a wide saddle, then swings to the left. The trail crosses an old road or two through here—just go across them. One of them runs alongside and below the trail to the left for a while as the trail drops on down the hill, past MILEPOST #105.

The trail goes through a rocky area, levels off and intersects a four-wheeler road at 105.2—TURN RIGHT and follow this on the level and basically straight. This is actually an old log road that was built to haul out trees from a timber sale here a few years ago. There is a creek running alongside on the left. At 105.4 the trail leaves this road TO THE LEFT, and heads on down the hill next to the stream and comes out to FR #149—TURN LEFT and follow this road.

When I came through here there was an old-style hobo living next to the road in a canvas tent. He was a quite nice older man, down on his luck, who was spending his time doing of all things hiking the Ouachita Trail. He would bag up all his equipment (had a cast-iron pot) and trudge along for a few miles, find a nice spot and set up camp for a week or two or three, and explore around. Then he would move on. He told me that he had planned to reach Oklahoma by the end of the summer (this was in March). He probably got more out of the Ouachita Trail than anyone who has ever hiked it!

The trail continues on the road. Rainy Creek is on the right, which is a good-sized stream with water all year, and even a swimming hole or two. The trail stays on the road until the bridge across Rainy Creek. Right after it crosses the bridge at 105.6, the trail leaves the road TO THE RIGHT, and heads out past a big cedar tree across a wonderful flat with great campsites—one of my favorite spots to spend the night. Harris Creek is on the right here, which flows into Rainy Creek near the bridge.

Just before the trail crosses Harris Creek, it intersects with a lesser forest road, #D87B at 105.8— TURN RIGHT and follow the road across Harris Creek. (This may be the last water source for a while, so you should fill up.) Stay on the road for about a hundred yards (go past a jeep road on the left), then TURN LEFT off of the road. The trail heads down through a flat that's got lots of ferns in it, past MILEPOST #106. Lots of good campsites here too, but it does get soupy during the wet season. Just beyond, the trail hits an old road trace—TURN RIGHT and follow it, past the end of a food plot off on the right. We will be on this old road for quite a while. It crosses a number of small drains, and Harris Creek comes alongside for a while at 106.3. There are a couple of long, straight stretches, and some rocky spots.

There is a lesser road that takes off to the right at one point—stay on the main road. Not too far beyond, at the beginning of another long, straight stretch, we pass MILEPOST #107. There is a big oak leaning all the way over the trail just beyond. The creek, which is now just a trickle, rejoins again for a moment, and the road begins to head uphill a little. Uh oh—this is not a good sign. The road winds on around up the hillside, past lots of reindeer. By 107.6 it is on top of the ridge, swinging to the left some, and still heading uphill. It does level off through a saddle, then heads back up again. There are several lesser roads that intersect here and there—stay on the main one, which is well-blazed.

It curves on to the right, still climbing, then crosses over the ridgetop and continues up the hill at a pretty good steady clip on the left side of the ridge. Along the way it passes MILEPOST #108. This is Suck Mountain. Hum, wonder where it got that name? Actually, this road is a pretty good way to gain this elevation (about 700 feet). And at one point on the way up during leaf-off, you can look to the right, over the top of the ridge, and see the very top of Round Mountain, which we will soon be heading over to. And off to the left across the hollow is Muddy Mountain.

The trail curves a little, then continues a straight, steep climb. It does finally level out some, which feels *real* good. (look for Suck Mountain Shelter at 108.6) At 108.6 the trail leaves the road TO THE RIGHT. It just bops up over the tiny ridge and drops back to the right down the other side and quickly levels. It is very rocky.

Round Mountain is again in sight just ahead. The trail swings away from Suck Mountain and heads through a long saddle towards Round Mountain. If you looked at the topo maps of this area, you could find a number of "Round this or that" mountains. They *are* kind of rounded off. Anyway, the trail here is very nice. There are some rock outcrops off through the woods to the right that may be worth a look-see.

The trail eases up a little out of the saddle, past MILEPOST #109, and curves to the left side of the mountain. Then it begins to drop on downhill, past a dry drain, then level through another saddle, then back downhill again along the left side of another hill, then level again. Lots of huckleberry. And moss-covered rocks. Down to the left is Bear Wallow Prong, which looks likes an interesting place to explore. Bear Wallow Prong? The trail continues on the level.

I just looked at the topo map (Story). You remember back a while when we would hike on the same mountain for twenty or thirty miles? You should see *this* map. Round Mountain. Brushy Mountain. Jeff Summit Mountain. Rainy Creek Mountain. Suck Mountain. Owens Mountain. Rocky Creek Mountain. Big Round Top Mountain. Little Round Top Mountain. Thorpe Mountain. Pot Mountain. Brantley Mountain. Kelly Mountain. Procter Mountain. Curtis Mountain. Phillips Mountain. And Chalybeate Mountain. Good grief! And all of these are right here within a mile or two of the trail. I like this kind of country. This would be a great area to set up camp for several days and just wander around. And you wouldn't need to worry about finding your way back to camp—it's just on top of that mountain…

The trail swings on over to another ridge and begins to head downhill some. It crosses another side ridge, then drops down to and through a saddle at 109.6, and heads up some out of it. The trail is working its way up the middle of the ridge now, then runs level for a little while, then slips down the left side of the ridge. It levels off some, through a rocky stretch, and passes MILEPOST #110. It goes through another saddle, swings to the right, then eases down some, but mostly level along the middle of the ridge.

The rises and falls through here are pretty gentle. And the underbrush gets a little thick here and there. We will be making our way across four of the mountains that I listed just up ahead—Rocky Creek, Owens, Big Round Top, and the longer Chalybeate Mountain. It's kind of hard to tell them all apart.

The trail runs level through another small saddle, then along the right side of the ridge, then rises up and levels again on the ridgetop. It eases down the hill to the left a little steeper than we have been doing, passing through yet another saddle at 110.8. This one is deeper than the others. You may see more of those faded yellow boundary signs along here. It heads on up the ridge, swings to the left and levels off.

Up on top, on the level, the trail passes MILEPOST 111.0. There is a nice view off to the right—you can see some of the other mountains that I mentioned. There is a large clear-cut area just down below, which is the reason for the open view. Before long these trees will grow up and obscure the view. We do need a few "controlled clear-cuts" once in a while—these are called vistas, and don't usually require cutting quite so many trees.

We come alongside the clear-cut on the level ridgetop, then ease up the hill. We swing to the left some, run level across the left side of a hill, then head back uphill. By 111.5 we pass through another saddle, then run along the right side of the ridge, downhill some. We cross an old grown-up road, then intersect with it soon after at 111.6—TURN RIGHT and follow this road.

The road drops into a small saddle, then just as the road heads *up* out of the saddle, the trail leaves the road TO THE LEFT. It heads up the hill at a pretty good clip, back and forth. Back and forth. There are some leaf-off views out ahead, and the trail finally does level off. The hillside is very steep, but the trail is in good shape. Just as we leave open hardwoods and enter a big stand of pines, we pass MILEPOST #112. And there is a leaf-off SSS view back to the left here.

The trail continues level, back into pines, merges with the ridgetop, then heads on downhill again to a saddle. Lots of huckleberry bushes. And good campsites. This is a long, narrow ridge. The trail picks up an old road trace and follows if for a while. Just as the trace heads up and to the right, the trail leaves it TO THE LEFT. The trail continues up the ridgeline, going on around the left side.

It heads on down the hill, which is pretty steep below, then levels and heads up some. This is nice, easy trail through here. It heads on uphill through the open woods, tops out on the ridge, crosses it at 112.7 (and the fence line again) and heads down the other side. There are a few good views out through the pine trees on this side of the mountain here and there. The trail rejoins the ridgetop and continues heading down. It passes through a saddle (good campsite, fence line again) at 112.9, then heads back uphill on the left side of the ridge.

It levels off and comes to MILEPOST #113. It remains mostly level for a while, crossing several dry drains, then heads up just a little. By 113.7 the ridge has come down to meet us at a saddle. There is an SSS view off to the right during leaf-off. The trail continues along the left side of the ridge, but it is climbing a bit, steep in a spot or two. Then level. There are a few big pines here and there. Some nice oaks too. And at 113.9, there are even some wizard oaks, which we haven't seen in quite a while. Welcome back guys!

The trail drops down just a little, then levels at MILEPOST #114. It remains level, and comes to a neat rock outcrop, and a trail intersection at 114.1. The Round Top Trail takes off to the right (white blazed), and heads 1.4 miles on down and connects with the Womble Trail right at the end of FR #D75A. We will connect with the Womble Trail ourselves in a little while. There is a pretty nice signpost here that has kind of a drawing of the area on it—you don't expect to see something like that way up here.

The OT continues STRAIGHT AHEAD, easing down the hill, through a saddle, then back up some on the left. It gets kind of rocky in spots. At 114.2 there is an SSS up on the right—a cave! Well, sort of. It reminds me of a sea cave. You could perhaps take shelter there during a rainstorm. Of course, keep in mind that places like that act as spark gaps when a bolt of lightening hits. Hum.

The trail rises up just a little along the side of the ridge, levels some, then begins to head on downhill. At 114.5 there is an SSS view as the trail comes to the end of the ridge and swings to the right. You can see most of the world off the end of this ridge, during leaf-off of course. It heads on down to another saddle, comes against the fence again, then swings on around the left side of the ridge, dropping slightly. There is lots of huckleberry. And lots and lots of thick, green moss. In fact, at 114.8 there are so many clumps of this magical stuff that I'll have to call it an SSS.

The trail continues easing down the hill, past MILEPOST #115. Then it heads uphill some. All of this ridge through here is Chalybeate Mountain. Actually, this is the second one in this section. We passed just to the north of another Chalybeate Mountain back at mile 105, west of Rainy Creek. Why would someone name not one, but two mountains names that you can't pronounce?

It drops on down the ridge some, past more reindeer and moss, then levels off some. By the way, you may notice spots along the trail where something has been digging into the side of the trail. These are usually armadillo dens. We seem to have gobs of them around these days. I remember only a few years ago when you never saw one. Now you see them all the time, sunbathing next to the highway. And once in a while you may even see one hiking the trail. If we could only figure out how to breed them with some of the most endangered species...

The trail does more up-and-downing, then the ridge comes down to meet us again, and we walk along it for a little while, past MILEPOST #116. It drops down just a little on the right side of the ridge. Some level. Past a number of big pine trees, and across several dry drains. The trail is in good condition. Soon you can look down and see a major dip in the ridge. And then Story Creek comes into view. What a nice sight!

The trail drops down to Story Creek at 116.7. (look for Story Creek Shelter at 116.7) This is a major feature of the OT. Upstream a ways is Chalybeate Spring, and lots of great camping spots. There is plenty of water here all year. A note of caution—treat **all** water out here in the wilds, *even* spring water. Spend some time here. Explore. Enjoy.

And rest up too, because from the creek the trail switchbacks steeply up the hill at a pretty good clip. This is the toughest climb that we've seen in a while. About half way up is MILEPOST #117. It does finally level out as the trail makes its way around the right side of McGill Mountain. It drops just slightly and intersects with an old road, and the Womble Trail at 117.2. This 38-mile trail takes off down to the right (blazed white), and is a pretty nice multi-day hiking trail. In fact, it is the third longest hiking trail in Arkansas (until more of the Buffalo River Trail is built). Guess what? You can find this trail detailed in my *Arkansas Hiking Trails* book. By the way, you can combine the Womble, Round Top and Ouachita trails and make a nice loop (accessed via FR#'s 231 & D75A down below).

The OT continues STRAIGHT AHEAD and along the road. It does some gradual up-and-downing, but mostly level. At 117.6 the trail leaves the road TO THE LEFT, and heads up a rocky hillside. It climbs across a steep hillside, past an "N" tree, levels some, then climbs steeply up again. It levels on top of the ridge at 117.9, is rejoined by the fence line, and continues along the ridgetop, past MILEPOST #118.

It slips on over the left side of the ridge, then turns and heads nearly straight down it. This is not too bad going down, but it is a real bear going up with a full pack. It soon levels somewhat across a side ridge, then heads down the right side of it. There is a neat boulder-strewn drainage back to the right that we will see a time or two on the way down. Which is exactly what the trail does—switchbacks down at a pretty good clip.

The trail finally hits bottom, turns right on an old road, and heads over towards a forest road. It leaves the old road trace to the right and intersects with FR #149 at 118.7—TURN LEFT and follow this road on over and across Muddy Creek. This is the same road that we crossed back at Rainy Creek. This is a good water source all year. If you are here in the summer, you should fill up your bottles, because the next reliable water may not be until Irons Fork, which is 10 miles away at 128.8.

Just past the far side of the bridge, the trail leaves the road TO THE RIGHT. There is a pretty good place to park here. It wraps around the left side of a wildlife food plot, crosses a couple of dry creek bottoms, then passes MILEPOST #119. This is real nice trail, running along just above the bottom. It swings to the left and crosses a creek at 119.2, then heads across a flat area and begins to climb the hillside, curving to the left.

Soon it switchbacks to the right, and begins a pretty good climb *up* Curtis Mountain, through a huge clear-cut area. This will not be a pleasant climb, but as you head up, the views behind you of McGill Mountain and beyond are nice. The planted pine trees are pretty thick, and growing up rapidly. You begin to get some idea of how vast this clear-cut really is as you wind up through it all. Just bow your head, follow your boots, and try not to think about it. Up and up it goes. Finally, at 119.7, you leave the clear-cut and enter the land of big trees and open forest once again. Thank goodness! The trail is still pretty steep, but somehow it's not quite as bad. It switchbacks up some more, then levels out on a hogback ridge at 119.9. This is Curtis Mountain proper.

The trail winds around to the right along the ridge, easing up maybe just a little, past MILEPOST #120. Lots of big trees. Beautiful, big trees. It does some up-and-downing, mostly along the ridgetop. At 120.7 it heads on down the right side of the hill, swinging a couple of times, down through a saddle. It continues down the left side of the ridge, past MILEPOST #121. It comes alongside Smith Creek and crosses it at 121.1. This is a fair-sized creek, but may dry up during the summer. There are some good campsites around.

It heads across the flat bottoms, then crosses a lesser forest road (D69). The trail heads up the hill just a little, runs on down to and across a tiny drain, then begins to head up the hill. It levels off, across another dry drain, then back uphill again. It makes one last run up the hill, past some nice pines, then comes out to Hwy. 27 at 121.7, and the end of Section Five. The trailhead is on the left just before you reach the highway.

The community of Story is about five miles south on Hwy. 27. There are a couple of little stores there, with gas, ice cream, sandwiches and a Post Office—zip is 71970. Since this is about the halfway point on the trail, it is your best bet for a resupply (send yourself a package addressed to Your Name, OT Hiker, c/o Postmaster, and state an expected arrival date). *NOTE: Bluebell Cafe/country store/shuttle and hiker heaven is here! 870–867–3999.*

SECTION SIX—17.1 miles
Hwy. 27 to Hwy. 298

Trail Point	Mile Point	Mileage West to East	Mileage East to West
Hwy. 27 Trailhead	121.7	0.0	17.1
John Archer Shelter	122.6	.9	16.2
FR #148	124.2	2.5	14.6
Sandlick Mountain	125.8	4.1	13.0
Bill Potter Shelter Spur	127.5	5.8	11.3
Irons Fork Creek	128.8	7.1	10.0
FR #78 North cross	133.6	11.9	5.2
Big Branch Shelter Spur	134.0	12.3	4.8
FR #78 South cross	136.1	14.4	2.7
CR #139/Tabor Mtn.	136.9	15.2	1.9
Hwy. 298 Trailhead	138.8	17.1	0.0

Section Six begins at the crest of a ridge on Hwy. 27, about five miles north of Story. All of this section is on the Jessieville Ranger District of the Ouachita National Forest. Their office is located in Jessieville on Hwy. 7. Quads are Onyx, Fannie, Steve, and Avant.

This is some of the best-built trail on the entire OT, with waterbars/dips that actually work. And there are a number of great vistas that have been cut out along the route. This District has also built a system of log shelters, and there are three on this section. The trail climbs up several mountains, but only a few really tough climbs. Most of this section is pretty gentle. Spectacular views at the vistas.

There isn't too much water during the dry season, except at Irons Fork, which is a wonderful spot seven miles in, and at the end of this section at the North Fork of the Ouachita River. Both are beautiuful streams and worth some time to explore. There are numerous other smaller streams along the way during the wet season though. There are a lot of nice oak trees here and there, but much of this section is through heavy pine forests.

Section six begins at the highway, which is mile 121.7. It runs along an old road for just a few feet, then leaves it TO THE RIGHT and goes to a trail register. It rises up just a little, crosses the log road a couple of times, and heads up the hill a little more. There is a giant pine tree at the second crossing. The trail is wide and smooth. It begins to switchback up the hill, and runs level past MILEPOST #122 near the ridgetop. It resumes climbing up the right side of the ridge, then swings back to the left through a rocky section and crosses it again.

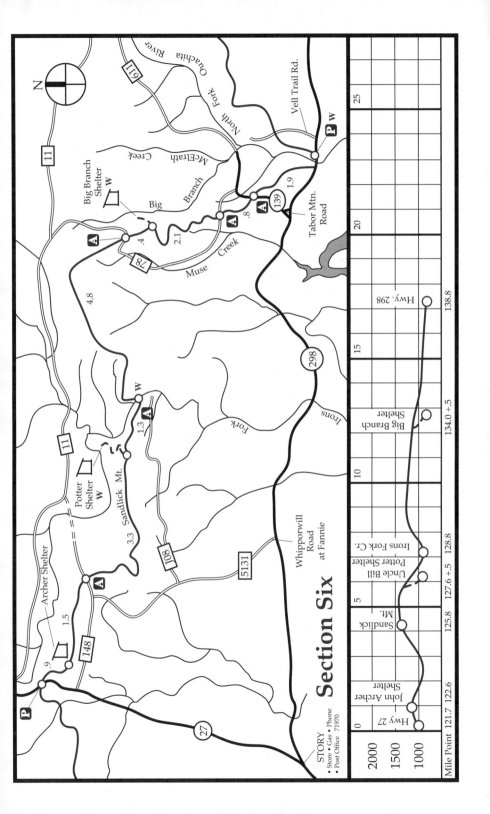

The trail runs level for a while along the left side of the ridge, and comes to the turnoff for the Ranger John Archer Shelter at 122.6. There is a sign here (short spur trail down to the left). These shelters are pretty neat, made of logs, and are equipped with a picnic table, fire grate and a broom (this one has a great view, but no water). The three-sided "AT"-style shelter has a solid floor and one open side. There is also a register, which often is filled with wonderful stories from grizzled trail hikers. John Archer, the long-time District Ranger of this District, is perhaps more responsible than anyone else for the success of the OT. He is a great trail advocate, and I hope that you meet him on the trail one day.

Some people love shelters. Some hate them. I think that they are pretty nice and have a place on this trail, as long as they are maintained and not trashed out by senseless folks (usually not hikers). There are a total of six shelters between this spot and Hwy. 7, but more are planned for other areas along the trail in the future.

From the shelter, the trail stays level for a little bit, then crosses over the ridge again on smooth trail through another rocky section, and runs along the right side, mostly level. It begins to drop just a little, passes a nice view to the right, then comes to MILEPOST #123. It continues dropping on down, past a huge oak tree that looks kind of out of place among all the pines. You will see a lot of tiny dips in the trail on this section. These are actually low-maintenance structures to divert water off the trail (to stop erosion), and they do work quite well.

There are a number of large pines along the trail as well, as it eases on down just slightly, nearly on the top of the ridge. It passes a small, dry pond that is down on the right at 123.5, then twists and turns on along. Nice, easy walking. The ridge is pretty broad, and there is plenty of room to camp. It dips down to and across a tiny seep, and heads on down the hill some more. You may begin to notice a fair-sized hill out in front across the valley—this is Sandlick Mountain, and yep, we will be up on it in no time.

The trail cuts a couple of switchbacks, passing MILEPOST #124, and continues swinging down the hill. Soon it hits bottom, passes through a thick area, then crosses FR #148 at 124.2 on an angle to the left. It eases down just a little more and picks up a road trace through a tall pine plantation SSS. These pines have been here a while. Imagine this place in a hundred years. Just beyond, it comes to and crosses a wet-weather creek at 124.3. If there is water here, it may be the last you'll see until Irons Fork.

Before long, as the trail eases uphill some, the old road trace sort of disappears underfoot, and the trail continues winding through the woods. It soon gets a little steeper, as it heads up a ridge, swinging back and forth across it. There are a number of road traces, and one of them is kind of washed out and resembles a ditch. The trail crosses it three times, and comes to MILEPOST #125.

The trail continues on up the hill, not too steeply, past another dry wildlife pond at 125.2 (the deer and turkey must be thirsty). Just beyond, the trail lands on the ridge that is Sandlick Mountain. It TURNS

LEFT and heads up the middle of the ridge. There are some nice views during leaf-off here. The trail is kind of steep and rocky, but just when the ridge gets *really* steep, the trail swings to the left and the grade eases up some. You are still climbing, but not near as much as you could have.

There is an SSS view back towards Hwy. 27 at 125.7 as the trail has leveled off somewhat. In fact, you can see a long ways back that direction. This would make a pretty good sunset spot. The trail continues to climb on around the left side of Sandlick Mountain, up some, not quite so up some, then more up. The trail is in pretty good shape, and it is soon running mostly level, on over to the saddle in the ridge that we could see from the trail a couple miles back.

It crosses an old road trace in the saddle at 125.8, and there is an SSS view off to the right, and to the left for that matter. You can see Lake Ouachita in the distance. There is a cleared out area to the right—this is used to land helicopters on by the Forest Service when fighting fires. The trail continues to ease uphill on the ridgetop, swinging to the right some, then left, past MILEPOST #126. It works its way around the left side of the ridge, rising up and down a little, but nothing too major.

You can look off to the left and see an honest to goodness river down in the valley—this is Irons Fork, and we are dropping on down the ridge to it. This is a beautiful ridge that we are following on down, if there is such a thing. The trail goes through a saddle of sorts (good campsites), then continues on down the left side of the ridge, past MILEPOST #127. It levels some, and actually rises ever so slightly, but generally is following the ridge on down towards Irons Fork.

At 127.5 is the intersection with the spur trail that goes down to the Uncle Bill Potter Shelter—it is on the left, and is blazed white. It's a half mile or so *down* to the shelter, which sits on a bench above Irons Fork Creek—a great place to go and stay for a night or two, with water nearby. There is a picnic table, fire grate and broom all ready for you. The climb back out is a tough one, so be prepared.

Just beyond the spur trail, the main trail swings on over to the right side of the ridge, rising slightly, then passes through another little saddle. Soon the trail is right on top of the narrow ridge, running down the middle of it mostly level. There is an SSS view off to the left at 127.9, especially during leaf-off. There are some nice, big oaks around just beyond. Just as the trail approaches an SSS area of tall wizard trees, it turns sharply to the left and heads steeply down the hill, past MILE-POST #128.

Soon the trail comes to a rocky gorge area out in front, and swings away from it to the right, and runs along mostly level. There are a number of big oaks scattered around through here too. It drops on down just a little as the hillside gets pretty steep. The trail is in good shape. Lots of wildflowers. It levels across a bench where there are some larger pines that join the oaks. Must be a reunion of old-timers. It picks up a mini ridge and heads down it—nice spot. Then the trail swings back down to the left, right, left and back right again. Left, right, and level just above a gorgeous pool area down on Irons Fork—

of course an SSS. Spots like this are common on the Ozark Highlands Trail, but not on the OT.

The trail makes one more little run down the hill and comes to a road intersection at 128.6—TURN RIGHT and head uphill on this old road (take the one that is more defined—there is also a lesser road off to the right). Just a little ways up the hill there is another road intersection—TURN SHARP LEFT and head downhill on another road (the road straight ahead at that intersection goes out to FR #J08, an access point). This road curves around to the right. There is a large, somewhat level bench up on the right that would make for good camping. Just as the road levels off, the trail leaves it TO THE LEFT and drops on down through a rocky area to Irons Fork at 128.8.

There is a wide, concrete walkway across this river. A most wonderful, super SSS. I would plan to spend a while here if you can. The water is terrific, of course, and there are a bunch of moss-covered boulders just upstream. Lots of water all year. Great for swimming. This is one of the largest rivers that we cross on the entire OT. It's one of those rivers that you can spend hours wading and exploring around in the summer. This is also the *last reliable water source for the next ten miles*, so be sure to fill up. Please re-read the last sentence.

Across the bridge the trail takes off TO THE LEFT through the rocks and heads upstream along the base of a hill. It comes through a neat rock outcrop on the right, then turns to the right and away from Irons Fork and heads up into a smaller drainage. It crosses an old road-bed and heads up the hill a little and alongside a nice small creek with several small waterfalls and pools.

The trail heads *up* the hill at a pretty good clip, past lots of huckleberry and reindeer, to MILEPOST #129. It continues up steeply, and is a real hump to get out of this drainage—should have stayed at the river or falls longer. At 129.2 it intersects with an old road trace and TURNS RIGHT onto it, levels off and crosses over a ridge. There is an SSS view here, an official "Vista" that has been cut out by the Forest Service. There are a number of these along this stretch, and they really open things up and give a spectacular view of the forest.

The road trace quickly begins to head up the right side of the ridge, and is a long, steady ridgetop-road climb up. It veers over to the left side, then the grade levels off some. It swings back to the ridge through a tiny saddle and begins another steep climb up the middle of it. It tops out at 129.7, runs level some through another saddle, then swings TO THE LEFT and leaves the road trace as plain trail.

The trail runs mostly level, and is in great shape as it crosses a hillside that is very steep up to the right. It quickly crosses a boulder field and comes to another SSS vista at 129.8. Terrific view back to the left. These vistas really add a lot to the enjoyment of the hike. From there the trail heads back uphill at a pretty good clip, then levels off and is easing uphill past MILEPOST #130.

It runs along level for a while, crosses an old road trace, past more reindeer, then picks up another road trace to the left and runs on over to a third SSS vista at 130.2. It's a spectacular view. You can see a

long ways into the mountains. If you are hiking west, those are the ba-
bies that you will be hiking through, so take a good look at them while
you can still breathe.

From there the trace runs mostly level along the ridge. Just as
the road makes a sharp turn to the left at 130.4, the trail leaves it TO
THE RIGHT. There is also a little spur trail here that heads over to the
left to another, perhaps the best and most open so far, wonderful, spectacular, SSS vista. From there the OT begins to head on down the hill at
a pretty good clip. It drops on down and levels off through a saddle and
comes alongside a forest road at 130.5, which is just through the woods
to the right. This road is not on the map.

The trail eases uphill some, still alongside the road, with a ridge
rising to the left. The trail grade is pretty gentle. It makes a little run
down through a small saddle and across an old road trace in it at 130.9,
then rises up again, away from the forest road. It turns into the hillside
and heads up a little steeper, past MILEPOST #131, and continues up
around the left side of the ridge. The grade lessens some, past lots of
huckleberry, then levels and even drops a tad. The ridge comes down
from the right to meet us and we run down the middle of the ridge for a
while, through a saddle, then back uphill some.

It drops down through another small saddle, then heads on up
the ridgetop a little along the left side. It climbs up past a neat rock outcrop at 131.5, then continues a fairly long and steep climb. It lands back
on the ridgetop, and follows it uphill a little more. There get to be quite
a few rocks around, but the trail is well dug out and smooth. The ridge
is very narrow, as the trail eases up the middle of it.

The trail heads through some thick underbrush, swings to the
right side of the ridge a little, levels off, and passes MILEPOST #132.
The ridge gets a little wider as the trail drifts across it again, rising up
now on the left side. It soon turns to the right at 132.3, crosses back
across the ridge just above a small saddle (good campsite), and begins
to head downhill some, following another ridge.

It goes through a rocky stretch as it continues to head down
into a saddle, then up the right side of the ridge. There is a large clear-
cut area off to the right through the trees. It opens up somewhat of
a view, but I sure don't like the price. There is a lot of private paper
company land in these hills, and many of the clear-cuts that can be
seen from the trail belong to them. But not all. The trail soon levels off,
then eases on down the top of the ridge some, through another saddle
at 132.7 (great campsite). As it heads up the other side there is an old
road that takes off to the left—be sure to stay on plain trail and up the
middle of the ridge.

It quickly levels off and passes MILEPOST #133, still on the
ridgetop. It winds on around through the pines, easing up a little, but
mostly level. A lot of the trail through here has been a pleasure to hike.
Gentle grades and great trail. Just as the trail breaks over the nose of
this ridge at 133.3, there is an SSS view out through the trees.

The trail switchbacks down at a pretty good clip, then levels
off and comes into a clear-cut area. It turns left for about twenty feet,

then turns TO THE RIGHT and heads on into the area. The trees were about 10–12 feet tall in 1993. There used to be a lot of these cuts made along this trail, and they were a real mess. But now we have the corridor protected and don't have to worry about/deal with new ones any more. Trail runs level through the clear-cut, out to and across FR #78 at 133.6 (also called Muse Creek Road).

This road seems to be traveled quite a bit. There is usually a hunter's camp off on the left. Lots of great camping spots as a matter of fact. It's a big, broad ridge. And the trail heads out across it on the level, past a wildlife pond. Soon we pick up an old road trace and it wanders across the wide bench and is easy to hike and follow.

This road passes a hillside thickly covered with huckleberry, and eases slightly up, passing a couple of dry drains, then comes to the spur trail on the left that goes about a half mile down to the Big Branch Shelter (blazed white). The trip down is not too bad, and the shelter sits in a wonderful location near Big Branch itself (i.e., water nearby). A picnic table, fire grate and broom are included at no extra charge. The trip back up to the OT gets a little steep, so get an early start.

Just beyond the spur trail is MILEPOST #134. And right after that, the road sort of ends, and the OT turns TO THE RIGHT and heads steeply up the hill.

The trail swings to the right and levels off somewhat as it crosses the left side of a steep ridge. You can look out across the valley and see a pretty good hill over yonder—this is Blue Ouachita Mountain, and yes the trail goes right up on top of it, and runs along it for quite a while. The Blue Mountain Shelter is up on top. But we'll save that climb until the next section.

The trail continues uphill some, and there is a view or two down towards Lake Ouachita. This steep hillside was covered with all kinds of different wildflowers when I was here in March. At 134.3 there is nice rock ledge just above the trail on the right. The trail crosses several dry drains as it heads on downhill some. There are some big pines here and there, and another rock outcrop.

It swings to the left some and runs along the side of a small ridge, mostly on the level. It drops down the right side of the ridge, past some cedars, then mostly level along the middle of the ridgetop. It picks up an old road trace there and follows it along on the level, through a rare area of briars. Then it turns to the right and begins to head *steeply* down the hill, leaving the ridgetop. There are some nice big trees at that spot.

On the way down, the road passes MILEPOST #135. And just beyond, the trail leaves the road trace TO THE LEFT, and continues as plain trail. It runs level through an area of real thick underbrush, then breaks out through a nice hardwood forest. It heads downhill some, back into pines, and bottoms out at a jeep road at 135.3—TURN RIGHT and follow this road for only about a hundred feet, then TURN LEFT off the road and head back into the woods.

It runs on a road trace from there, curving back to the left. The trace quickly forks—take the LEFT FORK and continue just barely uphill. It soon levels off, and runs through a low, mossy area that is kind of nice. Lots of reindeer here too. Pretty nice hiking. The road trace curves to the right some, past another mossy reindeer carpet. And there is a small wet-weather stream down to the left.

The road trace curves back to the left and more or less ends, and the trail continues curving to the left around the head of a holler. As it does so, at 135.7, I just can't stand it any longer, and have to name the reindeer lichen here an SSS—I've never seen so much of it—just covering the hillside! Clump after clump after clump. Lots of huckleberry too. Pretty neat stuff.

The trail does some up-and-downing, across the ridgetop, and past some private property off on the left (barbed-wire fence). Along the way we go through a saddle and pick up another faint road trace, and ease up the ridge, working around to the right, and head downhill a little. It comes alongside a small drain on the left, and passes MILEPOST #136. It continues down the hill and comes out to (through the fence) and across FR #78/Must Creek Road (our second crossing of it) at 136.1.

The trail continues through a level bottom area that gets grown up quite a bit with briars. It soon rises up a little, curves to the right, then picks up another old road trace and follows it TO THE RIGHT, and on the level. Good campsites. At 136.3 the road heads up a little steeper, and a lesser road takes off to the right—be sure to remain on the main road STRAIGHT AHEAD and up the hill. It soon levels off along the middle of a nice ridgetop. Wonderful hiking.

It begins to drop down the ridge a little here and there, and runs level some too, past an old home place on the left. The brush is so thick in there that I doubt even a snake could get through it. The trail skirts around it. Just beyond we step up and over a barbed-wire fence via a railroad-tie stile, and cross a paved road at 136.9—the trail crosses it on an angle to the right. This is County Road #139 (also FR #611, and marked on Hwy. 298 as Taber Mountain Road). There is another stile on the other side, and the trail takes off on plain trail, past a couple of dry drains, and MILEPOST #137.

The trail crosses several smaller drains, and curves around the hillside just below a large clear-cut up on the right. We've got some big pines along the trail. Towering trees. The trail just wanders around, swinging left and right, across several more drains, up-and-downing. At 137.3 it intersects with an old road trace and TURNS RIGHT and follows it on the level. Soon it goes through a low, soupy area, and then the road forks—take the LEFT FORK and continue along the road trace.

It remains on the road, which is pretty grown up. There is an SSS creek that comes next to the trail at 137.6—the banks along it are covered with moss. Not too large, but a pretty little stream. This area was protected from the clear-cut that ravaged the woods just above.

This is a lovely walk along the fern and moss-lined roadway. And the stream is still with us, but it is getting choked with briars and other thick stuff. At 137.9 the road forks—TURN RIGHT away from the straight road and head over to the creek and across on another road.

From there the roadway heads up the hill and splits for a moment, then comes back together. MILEPOST #138 is right there. The road continues up the hill, and just as it levels off, the trail leaves the road TO THE LEFT.

It heads up the hill some more on plain trail, then levels along a ridgetop. There are several open views across the way to Blue Ouachita Mountain. It just wants to remind us that it is up there. And waiting. At 138.3, as the trail makes a little run down the nose of the ridge, there is an SSS area where all the smaller trees, even a few of the larger pines, are covered with "Spanish moss," which is actually a type of lichen. Neat spot. The ridge here is a very narrow one. That's pretty neat too. The North Fork of the Ouachita River comes into view to the left for a moment.

Soon the trail makes a sharp turn TO THE RIGHT, off of the narrow ridge. It switchbacks down the side of the ridge, crosses a little creek, and heads on over to a registration box. It climbs over another fence just beyond, then up onto Hwy. 298—TURN LEFT here and follow the highway. It runs along it for about a quarter mile, crossing the N. Fork of the Ouachita River on a bridge (SSS rocks just downstream). It leaves the highway TO THE LEFT at 138.8 , where the trailhead is, and is also the end of Section Six. Hwy. 27 is 11 miles to the west at Story, and Hwy. 7 is 17 miles to the east at Blue Spring.

SECTION SEVEN—21.6 miles
Hwy. 298 to Hwy. 7 Trailhead

Trail Point	Mile Point	Mileage West to East	Mileage East to West
Hwy. 298	138.8	0.0	21.6
Blue Mtn. Shelter	143.2	4.4	17.2
Ouachita Pinnacle	147.0	8.2	13.4
FR #107	147.8	9.0	12.6
Blocker Creek	148.0	9.2	12.4
Big Bear Shelter	150.8	12.0	9.6
Old FR #107	153.0	14.2	7.4
Hoot Owl Gap	155.1	16.3	5.3
FR #122/Blakely Cr.	157.0	18.2	3.4
Moonshine Shelter Spur	158.4	19.6	2.0
Hunts Loop Trail	159.4	20.6	1.0
Hwy. 7 Trailhead	160.4	21.6	0.0

Section Seven begins at the trailhead on Hwy. 298, 11 miles east of Story, and 17 miles west of Blue Springs (on Hwy. 7). All of this section is located on the Jessieville Ranger District. Their office is located in Jessieville on Hwy. 7. Quads are Avant, Hamilton, Nimrod SW (just barely touches it), and Nimrod SE.

This stretch of trail begins as a lovely walk along the North Fork of the Ouachita River, but quickly climbs up onto Blue Ouachita Mountain, where it remains for quite a while, then goes up and down across several smaller ridges to the end at Hwy. 7. The views from up on the big mountain are terrific.

There is plenty of water the first mile, and then basically only one source (a tiny spring) for the next ten miles. Beyond that, water is adequate. There are three log trail shelters, which are great to spend the night at. There are a number of difficult climbs, most notably the main one heading up Blue Ouachita. All in all this is a pretty darn good section to hike at any time of the year, except, of course, in late summer.

 From the trailhead, the OT heads up the hill, through a split-rail fence, up and over a barbed-wire fence to a registration box—be sure to sign in. This is OT mile point 138.8. The trail soon tops out and begins a lovely walk on top of this big bench overlooking the river. Great campsites here on the right.

There are lots of big pines, and a few oaks. As the trail eases down slightly, it passes MILEPOST #139, and looks on down over the river. Soon beyond there is an SSS with another great view of the river, and lots of bearded trees hanging around. It is a sharp, steep drop-off

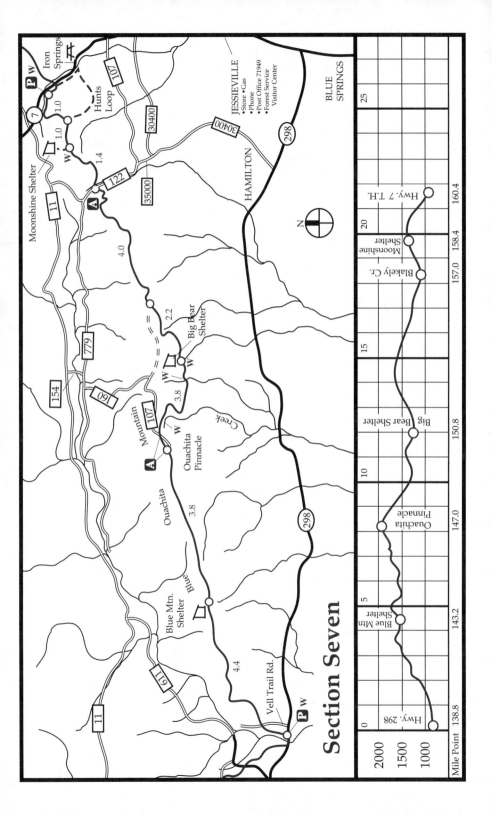

Section Seven

Map Labels

Iron Springs

P w

Hunts Loop

107

30400

JESSIEVILLE
• Store • Gas
• Phone
• Post Office 71949
• Forest Service
  Visitor Center

298

BLUE SPRINGS

HAMILTON

30400

7

1.0

1.0

1.0

w

Moonshine Shelter

11

122

35000

A

1.4

4.0

N

779

154

160

2.2

Big Bear Shelter

w

15

3.8

107

Ouachita Pinnacle

Mountain

A

w

Creek

Ouachita

3.8

Blue Mtn. Shelter

Blue

119

11

4.4

Vell Trail Rd.

P w

298

Hamilton

Elevation Profile

Mile Point	138.8		143.2		147.0	150.8		157.0	158.4	160.4
	Hwy. 298		Blue Mtn Shelter		Ouachita Pinnacle	Big Bear Shelter		Blakely Cr.	Moonshine Shelter	Hwy. 7 T.H.

2000

1500

1000

0   5   10   15   20   25

down to the river. Don't attempt to go down here if you need to right now—we will be pretty close to it before long. The trail continues along the top edge on the level. Lots of huckleberry on the flat. This is one of the most scenic little stretches on the trail.

It passes a rock outcrop that is down on the river, then runs on down to Vell Trail Road at 139.3—TURN LEFT and follow this road just across a creek, then TURN RIGHT and head up a lesser road. Back at the creek is the place to access the river. It is an SSS down there, and a great spot to stop and do whatever. This is the last reliable water source during the dry season for almost ten miles (to Blocker Creek), so be sure and fill everything up that you've got. There was a spring up on Blue Ouachita Mountain at the Blue Mtn. Shelter at 143.2, but most recent reports say there is seldom any water there now, so better to prepare for NO water at the shelter.

This jeep road heads steeply up for just a little bit, then tops out across a flat—lots of great campsites here, perfect for a large group. The road curves around to the right and drops down to another road trace at 139.7—TURN LEFT and follow the road a couple of hundred feet across a little drain, then quickly TURN RIGHT off of the road and head up the nose of a ridge on plain trail. There are lots more bearded trees— an SSS. Some of the beards come all the way to the ground.

It passes a survey monument just beyond and levels some, then lands on the right side of the ridgetop, past MILEPOST #140. It crosses a dry drain, easing uphill and swinging back and forth a little. We are beginning the climb up Blue Ouachita Mountain, a total elevation gain of over a thousand feet, that will end at Ouachita Pinnacle, the high point (half of that gain is in this next mile).

The trail swings back and forth across the ridge, leveling some as it does, and heads up at a pretty good clip on either side. You'll probably get to breathing pretty hard. It intersects an old trace at one point and TURNS LEFT onto it (and *up*) for just a few feet, then TURNS RIGHT off of it, past MILEPOST #141. It crests over the ridge soon after that and swings to the right along the left side of the ridge, and not near as steep. Edging uphill just a little, but lots of level too. There are some good leaf-off views out to the left of the Section Six part of the trail. And it passes an "O" tree. See if you can spot it.

The hill on the left is very steep as the trail works around a ravine, then the ridge comes on down to meet us, and we walk along it. The ridge broadens out and rises up some as we are now on the right side of it. You can begin to see Lake Ouachita off to the right through the trees. It swings back to the ridge, now narrow, and it heads uphill at a pretty good clip again. It's a steady but moderate grade, past MILE-POST #142.

It tops out and levels off a little ways beyond, running down the middle of the ridge. Then the ridge heads up again, and the trail stays with it. It tops out again at 142.6. There is a little spur trail to the right here that goes to a terrific SSS vista view—you can see Hwy. 298, Lake Ouachita, and the rest of the world beyond. A wonderful spot. You can also see all those clouds coming in—looks like rain. Where is that parka anyway?

From that spot the trail drops down the ridge, through a saddle, then veers over to the left side of it, levels some, then begins to rise just slightly past MILEPOST #143. The ridge widens out some, then the trail heads up more. It tops out at 143.2 at a spur to the left that runs on over to the Blue Mountain Shelter that is just down below the trail. It too has a picnic table, fire grate and broom. It was built in 1992 with the help of the Ouachita Mountain Hikers, the Wolf Pack Hiking Club, a Boy Scout troop from Hot Springs, and other volunteers. Be sure to sign the register there, and add your own little story if desired.

There was a shallow spring here that is accessed from the shelter or the trail. From the shelter, head on over to the right, just across the road trace, and you'll find it there. *Recent reports say this spring is DRY MOST OF THE TIME NOW and cannot be counted on for water.*

Back out to the OT now, which continues STRAIGHT AHEAD from the spur intersection. Just beyond this there is another fantastic SSS vista on the right. Really nice. And just beyond that is a faint spur trail to the left that heads on down to the spring. It was marked with a "Stream—300 feet" sign when I was there.

From that point the trail begins to head up the ridgetop, tops out and eases on down some, through a saddle, then up a little more. It swings off to the left side of the ridge. There used to be a sign here that pointed the way to Joe Noles Spring, 1/4 mile *down* the hill. That may be, but the hill is sooo steep here that I doubt you could ever climb back out. There were only rotting sign posts when I was here, no sign.

And from there the trail runs up the hill pretty steep, then levels some, and curves around the left side of the hill. Then it eases on down a little, then level, then down some more, past MILEPOST #144, which is right at an "N" tree. Then it comes to the edge and drops down the hill at a pretty good clip. There are a number of spots through here where you can look out ahead through the trees and see the ridge beyond.

After more steep downhill, the trail passes a rocky ridge up on the right, then goes through a saddle and heads up the hill a little on the left side of the ridge through a rocky stretch. It runs level for a while, then there is a long straight stretch of trail heading uphill—this is about the longest I believe I've ever seen through the woods on plain trail. It levels off at the end of it, and passes MILEPOST #145.

The trail remains mostly level across a steep hillside, past some big oaks. The ridgetop comes down to meet us once again, and we hike along it on the level for a while. Soon it begins to head uphill, gradually climbing steeper as we go along. I was breathing pretty hard on the tape. We join an old road trace and continue up, curving to the right just a little, past a stand of pines on the left. It soon levels off. We will be on this road all the way to Ouachita Pinnacle, which by the way comes into view out ahead—at least the antennas on top of it do.

The road begins to drop on down the top of the ridge, past MILEPOST #146. It levels off before long. There are some rock outcrops off on the right along here, and you could get a pretty nice view to the south from on top if you wanted one. The road eases on up the hill some, then runs on down the hill for a while, through an area of heavy briars, and wild plum (* see NOTE below). It levels off, then heads back up the hill towards the towers, past a bunch of ferns. Ferns? On top of a mountain? It gets kind of steep, then levels out just as the antennas come into view

The old road/trail goes over a hump in the road, and through a neat rock wall that circles this part of the mountain top, which is Ouachita Pinnacle. There is a giant antenna or two here, and an old fire tower site. You can get to this spot from Hwy. 7 via FR#11 (go 6.5 miles west, turn left onto FR#154, right on FR#779, left on FR#J60, which becomes FR#107 and ends). This is the highest that we've been on the trail for quite some time at 1961 feet. The last time we were up this high was back to the west of Hwy. 270, up on Fourche Mountain. And this is the highest point from now on for the rest of the trail. Does that mean that it's all downhill from here? Ha Ha. Want to buy some swampland?

The trail doesn't go all the way out to the road, it TURNS TO THE LEFT before it gets there and goes through the rock wall again to a trail intersection. MILEPOST #147 is there—this is where the trail reroute intersects. TURN RIGHT and you are back on the normal trail.

*NOTE: I'm going to confuse you here for a moment, sorry. A reroute leaves the road trace TO THE RIGHT, drops down and then levels out on a wide trail machine tread. This gradually eases up the hill and curves back to the left and across the old road just before it comes to the top of Ouachita Pinnacle. I prefer to just stay on the original road trace.

From MILEPOST #147 the trail heads on down the hill into the woods, swings to the right, then levels some. It quickly switchbacks down the hill, actually drops below a forest road just a little, then crosses FR #107 in a saddle at 147.8.

It picks up an old road trace there and begins to follow it down the hill. Blocker Creek comes alongside us down on the right—this is the first flowing water that we've seen since leaving the N. Fork of the Ouachita River. It will be with us for a while, and seems to run all year. If it is the dry season, you may not see water again until Hwy. 7. During normal times you will cross several more creeks. *If you are hiking west, be sure to fill everything up here.* The road trace continues down the hill some beside the creek, past MILEPOST #148.

The road drops some more, not too steep, even level here and there. It passes a couple of tiny springs that are choked with ferns and mosses. It curves back to the left (away from Blocker Creek) and right a few times, drops down to and crosses a couple of small drains. The first one had another small spring in it below the road. It makes a pretty good run up the hill, then levels and passes MILEPOST #149.

Just beyond this the road comes to an SSS on the right—a rock outcrop with a great view (you can just barely see the top of one of the towers back up on Ouachita Pinnacle). It turns to the left and heads down the hill at a pretty good clip. Just as the road turns sharply back to the right at 149.2, the trail leaves it on a lesser road TO THE LEFT, on the level. There is a pile of rocks at this corner that the famous Jim Rawlins piled up way back in the mid-eighties to mark the way. Be sure to follow the *blue* blazes.

This road trace remains level for a while, through a wet, seepy area, past an SSS view at 149.5. The road is grown up thick with brush. It begins to head down the hill, turning left, then right. At 149.8 there is a hump across the road, and the trail leaves it TO THE LEFT and heads steeply down the hill. It levels out a bit, then back downhill some to another road trace—TURN RIGHT onto this and follow it just a short distance to another hump across the road—TURN LEFT here and again head down the hill on just trail.

Pretty soon a creek comes into view down on the right. The trail levels off and heads into the ravine, passing MILEPOST #150. A nice campsite or two here. It crosses the creek at an SSS area (probably water here most of the time, except during dry months), and heads up and to the left just a little. The rocky trail crosses an old road trace and continues up the hill. It does some up-and-downing, and lands on another road trace and heads on the level for a while.

This trace slips on down and to the left a little, some level, across several dry drains, and comes to an intersection of sorts at 150.5—continue STRAIGHT AHEAD (maybe to the left a little) off of the road on plain level trail. As it heads on down the hill our next shelter comes into view down in the hollow. When I came through here all of this area for a while had just burned. The fire appeared to have killed some of the pines, but it was mostly a low fire.

The trail turns to the left and crosses the stream at 150.8 on a foot bridge. There is probably water here most of the year. The trail takes off to the left and comes to a road. The Big Bear Shelter is just up this road to the left. This one was built right in the middle of a rock field, and the area around it, especially right in front on the creek, is an SSS (a moss and fern-covered hillside on the creek). This is another wonderful log shelter, with a picnic table, benches, fire grate and a broom. It was also a joint venture between the Forest Service and several volunteer groups and individuals. By the way, can you guess how this shelter got its name?

For a bit of fun when there is plenty of water in the creek, hike upstream from the shelter along an old road trace and you'll find a pair of nice small waterfalls, each pouring into an emerald pool—all of it an off-trail SSS!

Back at the shelter, the trail crosses the road and joins another road that is heading up the hill. It swings to the right some and gets pretty steep. It winds around on up the hill, passing a number of boulder fields, to MILEPOST #151. It levels there some across the steep, rocky hillside. Just as it begins to head down the hill at 151.4, the trail leaves the road at a small hump TO THE LEFT and on the level for a few feet. It continues downhill, then eases up and swings to the left around a hill. There is a neat rock formation up on the left.

There are lots and lots of rock fields as the trail has swung around the hill and is mostly level on the right. It is dug out real well and has good footing. There is one SSS rocky area there that is covered with bright lichens and mosses. And the trail is about three feet deep through them. You may find that a rock or two has fallen back into the trail—if so, you should reach down and toss it back on the pile.

Just beyond, the trail heads back up the hill again. It swings over to the right some, levels off and picks up an old road. It weaves back and forth across the steep hillside, uphill some, then level through MILEPOST #152. It does some up-and-downing, still on the old road trace, then eases up the hill a bit. Eventually the trail leaves the old road TO THE LEFT at #152.5 and continues as plain trail, cutting across the hill.

At 152.7 the trail comes to and goes across a natural gas pipeline right-of-way. There is a great open view down the hill over the pipeline. Past the pipeline the trail goes across a couple dry drains, then rises up to what used to be FR #107 at 152.95 (the route has been closed off and is no longer a road). Go across the old road and ease down the hill just a little, through thick huckleberry and an SSS holly tree—the largest we've seen. Just beyond is MILEPOST #153. The trail drops slightly and makes its way along the left side of the hill, curving to the left some. It comes on around to the right, across a steep hillside, easing down some, past big oaks.

The trail does some up-and-downing, crosses a rocky dry drain or two, passes a dry pond down on the left, crosses a nice little spring drain area, then drops down to MILEPOST #154 on the level. Lots of huckleberry. And pines. It eases up the hill some, then down through a rocky stretch or two of poor trail. It picks up an old trace and continues down the hill on it for just a little bit, then leaves it TO THE RIGHT, and drops a little past another seep. Lots more huckleberry.

There is more up-and-downing across a number of dry drains that are choked with rocks and ferns. The woods are pretty thick. It passes MILEPOST #155 on the level, then drops on downhill through a saddle that is Hoot Owl Gap at 155.1 (it is customary for OT hikers to give a hoot here). I love owls. They look so neat. And you can often hear them calling to each other at night. You'll find them all along the trail. Actually, you'll find them up in the trees.

There are a number of old roads here, but the trail kind of splits them TO THE LEFT a little and heads out level on plain trail. The trail swings to the right some, drops down to a wildlife pond on the left in a saddle, and swings to the right away from it and across a road trace. It heads along the right side of the ridge, easing down some, then on the ridgetop a ways, past another saddle. It climbs some, swinging back and forth across and up the ridge at a pretty good clip to an SSS rock outcrop on top at 155.6. There is a nice, big, twisted pine there, and a great view.

The trail heads down the hill, switchbacking as it goes, then levels beside another saddle. By the way, there are good campsites in all of these saddles. It seems to me that there are so many saddles on this trail that we could start a horse ranch.

MILEPOST #156 is just beyond, and the trail continues on the level as good trail along the right side of the ridge. It goes through another saddle at 156.3 and intersects with a road trace there—TURN RIGHT and follow the road along the ridgetop. Before long the trail leaves this trace TO THE RIGHT and continues along the ridge.

It heads on down the hill on the right side, past a good view, then swings to the left. Lots of huckleberry, pine and dogwoods. Then it swings back to the right across the ridge and enters a clear-cut area. The trees were about 6–10 foot tall when I was here. It heads downhill and turns into the clear-cut to the left some. The trees get very thick, almost closing off the trail corridor. Then it exits the area to the left, across the ridge.

The trail heads on down the hill to FR #122 at 156.9. It crosses it on an angle to the left and continues on into the woods on the level, to MILEPOST #157. Right after, the trail crosses Blakely Creek on a little bridge. I've always found water here, but it probably dries up in the summer. If you are going to camp anywhere between here and Hwy. 7, be sure to fill up if there is water because you won't see any more until Hwy. 7 *(except for a pond that is near the next shelter)*.

The trail goes on up the hill, swinging back and forth, up steeply at times, then pretty gentle. It passes some large boulders as it continues to climb, some level spots. It heads downhill a little, across a couple of road traces, then level. And back uphill at a pretty good clip again. This isn't a pleasant climb with a heavy pack (never known one to be). It levels for a moment and passes MILEPOST #158, then resumes the climb, but not as steep. It finally reaches a wide ridgetop and levels off some—great camping.

It passes an "N" tree and a pond off to the left at 158.4, then swings to the right and comes to a road trace. The Moonshine Shelter is located to the left, less than a quarter mile along on this road. It is another wonderful log shelter, with picnic table, fire grate and a broom. I'm not sure if there is any moonshine. The only water there is from the pond though, so you might consider bringing some in if you don't have a filter.

The trail continues along the ridgetop, weaving around a little, on the left side of it, then on the right, then down the middle of it. It eases on down a little, past MILEPOST #159, then runs level again. It gets more serious about heading down now, back and forth to a trail intersection at 159.4. The Hunts Loop Trail (blazed white) takes off to the right here, and goes on over and down about two miles to the Irons Fork Recreation Area on Hwy. 7. It also runs along the OT for a while, then leaves it and loops back to Irons Fork, making a nice 4.2-mile loop trail. This is detailed in my *Arkansas Hiking Trails* book.

From this intersection, the OT turns TO THE LEFT and drops on down just a little. You will see some white blazes here and there for the Hunts Loop. It passes an SSS vista at 159.7 on the right, then eases up some, over a ridge and down the other side. It passes a wildlife pond on the right, across an old road trace, then comes to MILEPOST #160.

It continues down the hill through a saddle to the left, then past a nice SSS rock formation up on the right, and intersects with a road trace at 160.3—TURN RIGHT and follow this on down the hill. There are lots of reindeer around, and more rocks up the hill. It levels out at a registration box at 160.4. The parking area on Hwy. 7 and the end of Section Seven are just ahead across the Middle Fork of the Saline River.

The main OT does not cross here, but rather turns TO THE RIGHT at the registration box and follows an old road downstream, which is the beginning of Section Eight. This is also still the Hunts Loop, which continues on the road for 1.3 miles to the Iron Springs Recreation Area. This is a wonderful little picnic area right on Hwy. 7.

Hwy. 7 is a National Scenic Byway, and is in fact one of the ten most scenic drives in the United States—especially the part from Jasper to Russellville, and on down past the OT to Hot Springs. The OT trailhead is located six miles north of Jessieville, and a mile and a half north of Iron Springs Recreation Area (it is a large trailhead, and you can't miss it!).

SECTION EIGHT—27.0 miles
Hwy. 7 Trailhead to Lake Sylvia (FR #152)

Trail Point	Mile Point	Mileage West to East	Mileage East to West
Hwy. 7 Trailhead	160.4	0.0	27.0
FR #132	162.3	1.9	25.1
Sugar Creek	163.9	3.5	23.5
FR #153	165.4	5.0	22.0
Oak Mountain Shelter	167.4	7.0	20.0
FR #124	168.8	8.4	18.6
Green Thumb Spring	170.6	10.2	16.8
Grindstone Gap Spur	173.5	13.1	13.9
Creek	175.0	14.6	12.4
Crystal Prong Creek	177.2	16.8	10.2
FR #94	179.2	18.8	8.2
Flatside Pinnacle Spur	179.4	19.0	8.0
FR #805	179.8	19.4	7.6
Brown Creek Shelter	182.5	22.1	4.9
Brown Creek	183.1	22.7	4.3
N. Fork Pinnacle Spur	184.8	24.4	2.6
Lake Sylvia Spur	187.3	26.9	.1
Lake Sylvia	187.3 (+ .4)	27.3	.5
FR #152	187.4	27.0	0.0

Section Eight begins at the trailhead on Hwy. 7, six miles north of Jessieville, and a mile and a half north of the Iron Springs Recreation Area. All of this section is on the Winona Ranger District (once it crosses Hwy. 7). Their office is located on Hwy. 10 in Perryville. Quads are Nimrod SE, Paron SW, Aplin (just touches it), and Paron. Hwy. 7 is a National Scenic Byway, and is one of the Top-10 Scenic Drives in the United States. You will enjoy the drive to the trailhead.

This is one of the more notable stretches of the OT because it goes through Flatside Wilderness, was one of the first sections built, and is close to Little Rock. The trail climbs up and across several ridges, enters the wilderness area and stays high for a while along the edge of it, then drops down through the middle of it, across Crystal Prong, then up and out of the wilderness area over Flatside Pinnacle, then down into another big drainage, back up again to North Fork Pinnacle, then gradually down to Lake Sylvia. Lots of access points along the way.

Water is usually not much of a problem, although there are a few dry stretches. There are a number pretty good climbs, like up to both Pinnacles, but not too bad. The views, the wilderness, and the creeks make this section one of the most scenic parts of the OT. There are two shelters, one located on either side of the wilderness area.

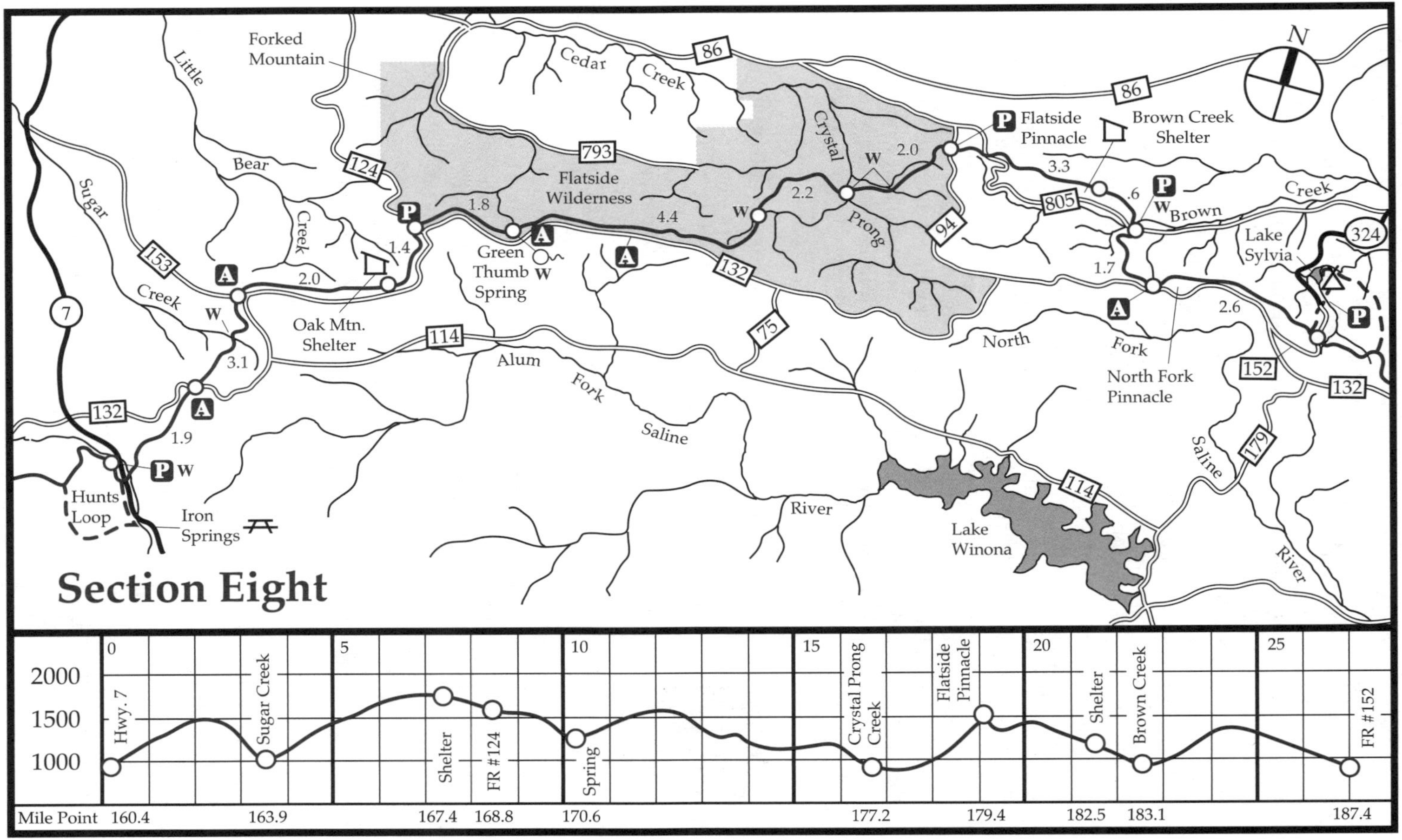

Section Eight
Forked Mountain
Little
Bear
Creek
Sugar
Creek
Cedar
Creek
Flatside Wilderness
Crystal
Prong
Green Thumb Spring
Oak Mtn. Shelter
Flatside Pinnacle
Brown Creek Shelter
Brown
Creek
Lake Sylvia
North Fork Pinnacle
North
Fork
Alum
Fork
Saline
River
Lake Winona
Saline
River
Hunts Loop
Iron Springs
N
86
86
793
124
153
7
132
132
114
114
75
94
805
324
152
132
179
2.0
1.4
1.8
4.4
2.2
2.0
3.3
.6
1.7
2.6
3.1
1.9
2000
1500
1000
Hwy. 7
Sugar Creek
Shelter
FR #124
Spring
Crystal Prong Creek
Flatside Pinnacle
Shelter
Brown Creek
FR #152
0
5
10
15
20
25
Mile Point
160.4
163.9
167.4
168.8
170.6
177.2
179.4
182.5
183.1
187.4

This section has special meaning for me because it was the first stretch of the OT that I ever hiked, back in 1975, and it was that hike that prompted me to write trail guides in the first place. I was teaching a backpacking class at the University of Arkansas in Fayetteville (at the ripe age of 19), and since there were no trails in the Ozarks to hike on, we went to the Ouachitas. I got a map of this section from the Forest Service, and that map showed the mileage for the trail from Lake Sylvia to Iron Springs to be 20 miles. Boy were they wrong! The mileage was 20 miles alright, but that was only for the *completed* trail, which ended after 20 miles on FR #132. It was still 12 miles from there to Iron Springs. Of course, what they had done was fail to tell me that the trail was not complete, and that it was 32 miles to Iron Springs. Well, I hiked that stretch, with a full pack, all in one day, all the way to Iron Springs (I was scouting the route for a class trip). It turned out to be the longest that I've ever hiked in a single day, with or without a backpack. Still is. And to top it all off, my freeze-dried-dinner bag broke open and spilled my only food all over the ground that night. Anyway, I decided right then and there that someday I would create a guidebook that would tell the correct story. The trail now, of course, takes a little different route, and doesn't even go on to Iron Springs, so the mileage is a few miles shorter. Live and learn.

 The trail is located just across a foot bridge over the Middle Fork of the Saline River from the trailhead. This is OT mile 160.4. Be sure to register at the box. The trail TURNS LEFT and heads downstream on a road trace. This is also the Hunts Loop Trail, which makes a 4.2-mile loop out of the Irons Fork Recreation Area. It will be with us for a short distance (blazed white). This trail is in the *Arkansas Hiking Trails Guide*.

The road soon heads up a hill, and just as it begins to get real steep, the trail leaves the road TO THE LEFT. It heads on down just a little, past lots of reindeer lichens, to a split in the trail. The Hunts Loop continues to the right and up the hill (1.1 miles to Irons Fork), and the OT goes down the hill TO THE LEFT. It drops down to and crosses the river, and actually goes under Hwy. 7 at 160.7. If the water is high, you can simply climb up on the highway and cross the river there.

On the other side, the trail heads away from Scenic 7 and goes up a hill into the woods. It runs along level for a while, across a couple of old road traces and small drains. Good campsites. It crosses another drain and rises up to MILEPOST #161. It continues up the hill, across another road trace, past lots of huckleberry. Soon it turns left at a drainage and heads right straight up the hill very steeply. This climb isn't too long, but it is tough. Before long it swings around a little bit and the grade lessens.

It tops out over a ridge at 161.5 and heads downhill some. There are lots of rocks around as the trail crosses another drain and eases up some. It swings to the left across another ridge, then drops on down across another drain, then levels to MILEPOST #162. It eases up through some rocks a little along the right side of a ridge. Some up-

and-downing. Then rises up to and across FR #132 at 162.3. This road is the major route through this stretch of the National Forest, connecting Hwys. 7 and 9, and is known as the Winona Forest Drive.

The trail curves on to the right as it heads uphill, swinging back to the left, then down a little, and level. It picks up the pace downhill again, then levels through a saddle. Lots of big oaks. It rises up a ridgetop, and tops out at MILEPOST #163. It begins to head on down again, to the left some, across another ridge. You may have noticed that the waterbars across the trail on this side of Hwy. 7 have been different—these are usually rock instead of just a dip in the trail, and they usually don't work. In fact, a lot of them are simply in the way. Each of the Ranger Districts does their part of the trail a little differently.

The trail continues down the hillside, across another small ridge or two. It kind of doubles back to the right, down to and across a road trace and levels in the bottom. There are some good campsites down here. It swings to the left and crosses Sugar Creek at 163.9. There is probably water here most of the year. You may not see water again though until Green Thumb Spring at 170.6. The trail TURNS LEFT onto an old road for just a few feet, then leaves it TO THE RIGHT and heads up the hill, across a smaller side drain.

It turns to the right and heads up this little drainage. All of this section for a ways up the drainage is an SSS—it's a beautiful little stream, that tumbles down the steep hillside. There are lots of rock outcrops, moss-covered ledges, and little waterfalls—including Sugar Falls, a nice ten foot tall waterfall. The trail is steep, as it goes right up alongside the creek, but it doesn't seem to matter. Someone built this part of the trail in the right spot. Just lovely!

In the middle of all this is MILEPOST #164. Soon after, the trail crosses the creek and heads up the hill to the right, leaving this wonderful spot. It gets kind of steep for a short run as it curves back to the left, then passes under a powerline. It levels some, then eases up a little more. At 164.5 the trail turns to the left and crosses the head of our little stream again, then eases on around the hill to the left. It does some up-and-downing, across several dry drains, as it is working on around the edge of a hillside.

It crosses a road that leads to a food plot to the left at 164.8, and continues straight ahead. The powerline is off to the left as well. The trail eases up some more, past MILEPOST #165, and around to the left a little, across rocky hillside. It approaches an old road trace, but swings to the right away from it and continues to head up the hill, a little steeper now. It's rising up the right side of the ridge, and FR #132 comes into view down on the right.

The trail drops on down to and across FR #153 at 165.4 (FR #132 is just off to the right). There are actually two roads here, and one of them is gated. The first one is FR #153, which we do cross, then we go along the gated one for a few feet then turn TO THE RIGHT off of this road (before the gate) and head down the hill into the woods. The trail runs across a steep hillside, but is mostly level. It's a little rocky here and there, and there are a few pines around. It does rise up just a little past MILEPOST #166.

It crosses a couple of road traces, rising ever so slightly, and is kind of rocky. There is a spot or two that is grown up with briars. At 166.4 there is a faint trail that heads back to the right—it goes up the hill to FR #132 and is seldom used. The OT continues STRAIGHT AHEAD, running mostly level as it winds around across the hillside. It swings to the left and down a little across a pine-covered ridge. It crosses an old road trace there (that runs on out to the point). The trail swings on down some more to the right through a real rocky area, then runs level, past MILEPOST #167.

The trail heads on up a little, next to the forest road, then heads up a little steeper. It hits an old road trace at 167.2—TURN LEFT and continue heading uphill at a pretty good clip. It swings to the right, then near the top comes to the Oak Mountain Shelter Spur at 167.4. This shelter is just down the hill to the left. Nice leaf-off sunset here, but no water. Just past the spur, the trail leaves the road TO THE LEFT. There is an old fire tower site off to the right here on top of the hill.

It was raining hard when I came through, and I was thrilled to find an old latrine over there. It had a cement seat, but the roof kept me dry as I used it for my office to plan my next few miles. The little shed was rotting away though, and has long since disappeared. Just in case you were wondering where all of the towers went, they were sold and hauled off years ago and replaced by spotters in airplanes which are supposedly more efficient (but much less romantic).

By the way, the mountain that we have been hiking along for a while is Oak Mountain, and we will soon be joined by White Oak Mountain. Off in the distance are Red Oak, Pin Oak, Chinkapin Oak and Blackjack Oak mountains (just kidding).

Back at the road intersection, the trail heads down the hill at a pretty good clip. It swings to the left some, and levels, and crosses a couple of dry drains at the head of a deep hollow (this eventually forms Little Bear Creek). Then it heads back up the hill, across a ridgetop, down the other side, then back up again past MILEPOST #168. It goes across a rocky hillside, mostly level, then crosses a road trace and resumes up a little, then level for a ways. It rises some more, crosses another trace, then level again.

There are a few views out through the trees during leaf-off, but I can't give you any details because I couldn't see much through the rain. The trail comes to and crosses FR #124 at 168.8—there is a small trailhead parking area. You are now inside the Flatside Wilderness Area, a wonderful 9,507 acre tract of ridges, rocks and streams. It was designated as Federal Wilderness in 1984. I am proud to have been one of the many who trudged to Washington to testify at the Congressional hearings to get it established.

The trail drops just a little and curves to the right, past a registration box, and continues down the hill some to MILEPOST #169. Things get kind of rocky for a while, and the trail enters a pine forest for a little bit. Lots of mosses and huckleberry bushes. It does some up-and-downing across the steep hillside, then runs along a level rocky bench at 169.4. It was at this point on this hike that I first got a glimpse of Forked Mountain rising out of the mist.

You can't mistake this mountain for anything else. It does "fork" at the top, and one of the peaks is shorter that the other. Wyoming has the Tetons. Arizona the Grand Canyon. Alaska has Mt. McKinley. And the Ozarks have Hemmed-In-Hollow and White Rock Mountain. Like all of those magical places, Forked Mountain is very special indeed. You can tell that just by looking at it across the way. It is my favorite spot in the Ouachita Mountains. The OT does *not* go to it, but you can drive nearly to the top for easy access. It reminds me of the high mountains in the west, with its incredible boulder fields and spectacular views. And, there is a cave up on top. I spent one wonderful night inside it many moons ago during a terrible downpour. I'll take you there sometime. You will be seeing this special place off in the distance a lot as the trail goes on. It is a quiet sentinel sent here to watch over the wilderness.

The hillside gets steep again, and the trail does more up-and-downing across it. All of the trail through here for a while is running just to the north of, and down below FR #132. The trail climbs on up a little, crosses an old road trace near an open spot at 169.9 (perhaps an old homesite), then tops out and swings away from the open area and heads back down some again, past MILEPOST #170. It actually heads towards the forest road, then swings away from it to THE LEFT, down the hill, then back right again.

The trail is mostly level for a while, on top of the broad ridge and on the left side. Soon it begins to drop just a little, comes to a small stream, then heads down alongside it. At 170.6 the trail crosses this stream and comes to Green Thumb Spring (it runs into a little pond that normally has water). There is an old road trace there that heads up the hill to the right to FR #132, and is a good access point for the OT.

The OT crosses that road trace and continues along on the level. It crosses several dry drains and heads up the hill some, past MILEPOST #171. After that it switchbacks up the hill pretty steeply. It climbs up to the left, across more dry drains. There are lots of blackjack oaks around. And lots of rocks. The trail is in pretty good condition as it continues up the steep hillside. It swings back to the right and levels out some on a ridgetop at 171.5. It crosses the ridge, then rises up some.

It winds on around a bit, and comes to an SSS open view at 171.5—Forked Mountain is right in the middle of the picture. A good campsite too. In fact, from now on for a while there are lots and lots of good sites. The ridge is broad as the trail runs mostly along the middle, then along the left side some, past MILEPOST #172. This is White Oak Mountain. And the hike along it is pretty gentle. Open woods, mostly flat. The trail eases up ever so slightly, curving to the left some.

At 172.5 it begins to head on down the hill, swings back to the right, and passes MILEPOST #173. You begin to get some views here and there through the trees of Flatside Pinnacle, which is out ahead, across the wilderness. We'll be heading up that way after a while. It's mostly level now for a while, with a little up-and-downing.

At 173.5 there is a trail intersection. The spur trail to the right goes on up to Grindstone Gap on FR #132, and is another good spot to access the OT, but isn't used much.

The OT continues STRAIGHT AHEAD, out through the mostly level pine forest. Lots of huckleberry. It curves to the right, past a wildlife pond at 173.7, and a number of big oaks. It rises up some, following a rocky ridge off on the right, past MILEPOST #174. It crosses a ridge of thick pines and brush on the level, then heads on down, swinging left and right. It crosses a number of dry drains. Mostly level for a while. Lots of small wild iris wildflowers in the drains. The trail gets kind of rocky as it crosses more tiny drains, now bursting with iris. And the trail continues to make its way on down the hillside.

All of those drains that we've been crossing do gang up and combine to form a nice little creek down on the left at 174.7. And soon the trail comes alongside and crosses the creek at 174.95, then turns right. There is a neat rock formation that has cropped up on the left—an SSS. MILEPOST #175 is there, just before the trail heads up and around the end of the outcrop. There are several holly trees around, which really stick out during the leaf-off season. The trail runs along the creek, across the end of a couple of rock slabs, which can get pretty slick when wet.

Just beyond is a terrific SSS right on the creek that is called Moccasin Springs. Several little slough falls and rock formations. Really nice. The valley is pretty tight here. This creek flows into Crystal Prong, which we will cross later. From this spot the trail heads on up the hill, past a spur trail that goes down to a campsite on the right, then levels off. It goes through a real bad rocky spot, mostly level, and leaves the creek area. Just a note here—from the topo map it looks like there might be some neat stuff on this creek downstream a ways—if you camped in the area, you should explore and see what you find.

The trail remains mostly level, swinging back to the left across a broad ridge. Lots of good campsites. It begins to ease up some, along the left side of a rocky ridge, past MILEPOST #176. It levels some, across a dry drain or two, and past lots of huckleberry. Then it turns right, crosses over the ridge and begins to head down. It runs mostly level across a steep, rocky hillside. Big pines here and there. The trail gets kind of rocky. At 176.6 it levels and passes high through a saddle—good campsites—then resumes heading down some to the right.

The steep hillside that the trail crosses now is home to lots of ferns and iris. And the understory is choked with dogwoods. It's so bright and thick when they are all in bloom, you can hardly see. This is a very pleasant hike. Some big oaks. And a holly tree. The trail crosses several deep but tiny ravines as it runs level some, but gradually downhill.

At the MILEPOST #177 area a number of holly trees have joined the mix. Now that is something that the Ouachitas have that the Ozarks don't, and I like 'em. In fact, there are so many of them here, we'll just have to call it an SSS. There is a giant oak on the right too.

Soon after, the trail heads down a flight of steps, across an old road trace, through a muddy area, and comes to Crystal Prong Creek at 177.2. This area has been overused in the past, and you will see a number of campsite areas worn clear of brush here. I guess it is best to camp where the area has already been impacted, but I would prefer to go somewhere else altogether and find a more private spot to camp.

NOTE: This area was hit hard by a severe storm in 2011 that destroyed part of the trail so be alert to changes in the route.

There is a good spot or two to swim, and the water is here all year. An SSS of course. There are some neat rocks sticking up out of the creek. The trail crosses the creek (could be a wet crossing during high water) and continues mostly on the level, and just above the bottom. There is ample camping on both sides. Soon the trail turns to the right and begins to work its way on up another branch of Crystal Prong. Nice walking all through here.

The trail swings away from the creek just a little, crosses a little spring area that is full of moss, then swings back to the creek. It eases up onto a bench at 177.7 that overlooks the creek for a short distance, then comes back down to the creek again. It runs along the base of the hill on the right, which is covered with ferns and mosses. This little valley area is an SSS. A real nice walk.

This stretch of the trail all along here does get quite a bit of use, especially on spring weekends. Spring is one of the best times to be here for sure, but you should try for midweek when you would have the place to yourself. Of course, I might show up.

The trail veers up to the right again, then returns to the creek. At 177.9 the creek forks, and the trail crosses one of the forks. Good campsite here. It heads up the hill across an old road trace, then up a flight of steps. It swings to the left, past MILEPOST #178, then heads steeply up for a little while. The hillside is really steep, and covered with huckleberry. The trail continues up and around the hill, but not too steep now. Then it soon drops down and comes alongside the creek for a while, running mostly level. At 178.4 it crosses the creek and begins a pretty good climb up and out of the area.

It's a steady climb up on good trail, then it switchbacks up steeply for a short spurt, up to an over a narrow rocky ridge at 178.9. It passes a frog pond just beyond, then follows along beside the rocky ridge up the hill to the right, past MILEPOST #179. From there it climbs on up pretty steady, to a registration box, then turns to the right and heads up a flight of steps to FR #94 at 179.2. There is a parking area there of sorts, which is used mostly by folks hiking up to Flatside Pinnacle, which is just exactly where we are headed. There is a pretty nice view from the parking area, but it gets better. Much better.

The trail crosses the road and curves to the left, going underneath a stone monument to Senator Dale Bumpers who did so much to help establish Arkansas wilderness areas in the early 1980's (a short spur to the right leads to the monument). The trail continues up and turns right as it climbs, then runs level just a little. At 179.4 it comes to a saddle and a trail intersection. The spur to the top of Flatside goes to the right a couple hundred yards up to it.

It is almost mandatory that all OT hikers take this spur (drop your pack here if it's heavy like mine always is). The view is nothing short of spectacular. And the sheer rocky hillside is pretty nice too. This is a good spot for the sunset, especially in the winter when the sun is more to the south. You've basically got a view out across the entire Flatside Wilderness area—Forked Mountain sticks up in the distance, still standing guard. And you can look over to the left and see North Fork Pinnacle too, which we will be climbing up to after a while. It is kind of narrow on top, and the footing can get tricky, so be careful.

Back down at the spur intersection, the OT goes straight across the saddle (be sure to follow the blue blazes), and eases down the hill some. It gets a little steeper, passes a rock outcrop or two, crosses over the nose of a ridge to the left, then switchbacks down further to and across FR #805 at 179.8. The trail drops a little after the road, past a pond on the left, then it turns to the right and heads steeply up the hill, past MILEPOST #180.

From there the trail climbs up a little more, curves to the right, then left over and around an SSS rocky ridge, and begins to drop down the other side. Pretty nice views. The trail gets a little rocky, levels out through some scrub blackjack oak, then climbs up to the left some, and levels across the ridge at 180.7. It continues to rise a little on the left side of the ridge, then crosses a flat area, past MILEPOST #181.

The trail begins a long run down the side of the ridge, then levels along the top of it. It eases up along the left, then crosses the ridge and heads downhill again. It levels at a neat SSS rock outcrop that is covered with thick moss and reindeer. Come to think of it, so was most of the hillside. Soon the trail heads on down, swings to the right past MILEPOST #182.

The trail runs mostly level for a while, weaving back and forth across a broad ridge, them comes to the spur to the Brown Creek Shelter at 182.5. The shelter is just off to the right in a beautiful spot. If there is plenty of water flowing in creeks, there is a small waterfall and stream about 200 yards to the southwest from the shelter.

From the shelter spur the trail begins to ease on downhill, then makes a few switchbacks, heading towards Brown Creek. There are some big trees, and a hillside or two of ferns along the way. It runs down a short flight of steps and lands in the bottom. It stays there for a little ways, passing MILEPOST #183, then turns to the left and goes over to and across Brown Creek on a wooden bridge at 183.1.

All of this area in here is easily accessible from the forest road that we are about to cross, and so it is heavily used. There are lots of campsites around though. There is water here all year. From the creek, the trail goes on over to a registration box, then crosses FR #805 (there is somewhat of a parking area here). It turns to the right just a little and begins to head up the hill. Uh oh.

It switchbacks up the hill at a pretty good clip. Not much fun with a heavy pack. It passes under a rock outcrop at 183.5, then climbs a little less steeply. It tops out on a small ridge and runs along it for a little while, then continues *up* the hill. It passes an SSS rock outcrop off on the right, crosses an old road trace, then rises up to MILEPOST #184. From there it makes another steep run up, then levels off somewhat.

The trail is running along the left side of the ridge. It heads up the hill some more, past a number of large oaks, across the rocky hillside. The trail itself is in pretty good shape. The leaf-off views are getting better as we go up. You can look back and see Flatside Pinnacle. It passes some neat rock formations at 184.4, then switchbacks up the hill a couple of more times..

It finally levels off and comes to a trail intersection at 184.6. The spur trail goes to the right up to an access on FR #132. The OT continues STRAIGHT AHEAD and on the level, then easing up, making its way along just down below some nice rock outcrops up on the ridge. It heads on up to another trail intersection at 184.8. The spur to North Fork Pinnacle heads steeply up the hill to the right, intersects with an old road, then follows it to the right up to the top. There is a pull-off on FR #132 at the other end of this road. I prefer the view from Flatside Pinnacle though.

From trail intersection, the OT continues STRAIGHT AHEAD, along a rocky route that begins to drop down the hill and head toward Lake Sylvia. It passes an "N" tree on the way down, and MILEPOST #185. At 185.4 the trail levels off and swings to the left past a wildlife pond. It passes a couple of rock formations, does a little up-and-downing, and goes across a side ridge, past MILEPOST #186.

The trail runs level for a while, crossing an old trace at 186.2. This old road swings on down the hill and eventually ends up at Lake Sylvia, and used to be the old trail route. Was this the way I hiked on that fateful day back in March of 1975 on my 32-mile day? I've tried to forget that day ever since, so I can't tell ya. Anyway, soon after that the trail comes around another side ridge, and Lake Sylvia does come into view off in the valley below. You know something—this is a nice, gentle, pleasant hike.

The trail now begins a pattern of crossing in and out of quite a few little rocky drainages, many of them full of moss, ferns and wildflowers, and each one a treasure. Up and down. In and out. Lots and lots of tiny drains. Gradually heading on down the hillside. Past some nice trees, and gobs of huckleberry. Lake Sylvia is a ways off now.

It passes MILEPOST #187 and continues on. There are some areas that are pretty rocky, but the trail is in good shape. At 187.3 it comes to a trail intersection. The trail to the left goes on down to the trailhead parking lot at Lake Sylvia—it's about 4/10's of a mile. If you are ending your hike here, this is where you want to go. This short piece of trail is part of a 4.2-mile loop trail that leaves from the same parking area, runs along the OT for a while, then branches off and loops back to the trailhead (described in *Arkansas Hiking Trails*).

Back at the trail intersection, the OT continues STRAIGHT AHEAD, curves to the right a little, then drops on down to FR #152 at 187.4. This is the end of Section Eight. The trailhead at Lake Sylvia is about a half mile to the left. (To get there, take Hwy. 324 from Hwy. 10 for about four miles, past the campground to the trailhead.)

SECTION NINE—14.6 miles
Lake Sylvia (FR #152) to Hwy. 10

Trail Point	Mile Point	Mileage West to East	Mileage East to West
FR #152	187.4	0.0	14.6
Chinquapin Gap	188.7	1.3	13.3
Nancy Mtn. Shelter	189.5	2.1	12.5
Hilary Hollow	190.0	2.6	12.0
Hwy. 9	191.8	4.4	10.2
USFS Boundary	192.5	5.1	9.5
Pipeline Cr., 1st cross	193.1	5.7	8.9
Maumelle River	195.6	8.2	6.4
Red Bluff Creek	196.3	8.9	5.7
Hwy. 10	202.0	14.6	0.0

Section Nine begins just south of Lake Sylvia, a nice Forest Service Recreation Area. To get there, take Hwy. 324 off of Hwy. 10 for about four miles. The trailhead is located on FR #152, just past the campground on the left. The first five miles of this section are on the Winona Ranger District (office in Perryville). The rest of the section is either on private land or Central Arkansas Water property (also within the Maumelle River Wildlife Management Area), and the trail is managed by Pinnacle Mountain State Park—*Note: NO CAMPING is allowed after mile 192.5.* The quad maps are Paron, Fourche SW, and Martindale.

The first six miles of this section go through typical Ouachita forest, with lots of ups and downs (but nothing too severe), through Hilary Hollow, one of the most scenic walks on the trail. The rest of the section is in the flat bottoms, running alongside the Maumelle River. Most of it is a cake walk. There is plenty of water along the way. And there is one trail shelter, the last one on the OT—the Nancy Mtn. Shelter (which was burned by a stupid redneck in 2005, but was replaced in 2006 thanks to the forest service and FoOT volunteers).

There may be changes to parts of the trail in this section that run on private land (fewer or more bridges, short reroutes, etc.) Before hiking this section it is a good idea to check the **FoOT** web page for the latest information (www.friendsoftheouachita.org).

 There is a spur from the trailhead that crosses the forest road and heads on uphill and intersects with the OT— TURN LEFT here. The trail runs back over to the forest road, crossing it and officially beginning this section (which is about a half-mile from the trailhead). The mileages listed above show the distance to/from this road. This is OT mile point 187.4.

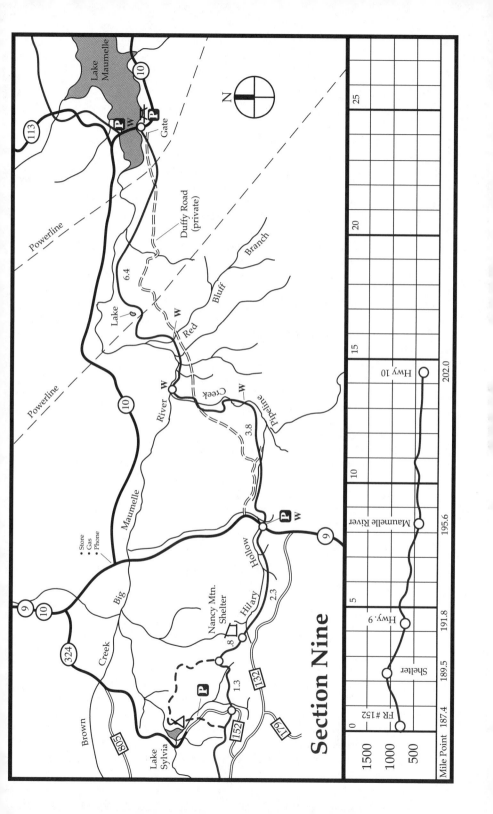

Section Nine

The trail eases on down the hill just a little, swinging to the right, across several tiny drains. It crosses a creek at 187.6 and swings back to the left. It remains mostly level, past several holly trees, some big oaks and pines too. It weaves around at the base of some small ridges, across a large flat, past MILEPOST #188. Just beyond, the trail heads up a little ravine, following a small creek, easing uphill.

At 188.5 the trail swings to the left and crosses the stream, and heads uphill some. It soon levels off and comes to a trail intersection at 188.7. This is Chinquapin Gap. The trail that goes to the left is part of the Lake Sylvia Trail (detailed in my *Arkansas Hiking Trails* **Book**). You can take this trail down to Lake Sylvia and back to the parking lot for a total loop of 4.1 miles. The OT continues STRAIGHT AHEAD.

It eases up the hillside, swinging to the right. During leaf-off you can look ahead and see Nancy Mountain (no, we're not going to climb it). The trail soon passes MILEPOST #189, and continues easing up the hill, around to the right, past a huge pine tree, and across a steep hillside. At 189.5 the trail levels off as it goes through a saddle. The Nancy Mountain Shelter is located just off the trail to the left here.

Beyond the shelter, the trail quickly drops into a neat drainage called Hilary Hollow (named after a friend of mine from Colorado), and we'll be following it all the way to Hwy. 9. I would vote this stretch as one of the most enjoyable hikes on the entire trail. I think I'll call it an SSW—Special Scenic Walk. The trail crosses a couple of small drains, past a rock field that has tufts of thick moss growing up between the rocks. Heavy huckleberry hillsides and lots of pine. It crosses the face of several little finger ridges as it continues down the hill. The whole area is lush with lots of ferns and wildflowers. There is one stand of cinnamon ferns along the trail that grows five or six feet tall!

The trail levels off a bit and passes MILEPOST #190. There is a small stream off on the left that we've been following—it will get larger as we go along, but we won't cross it. The trail continues to ease downhill through several small drains, then runs along the flat bottom for a while. Did I say that this was an enjoyable hike? The valley narrows somewhat at 190.6, and the trail runs along above the creek, looking down on it. It crosses a larger side stream at 190.9, where things get a little rocky, then passes MILEPOST #191 on the level beyond.

During the springtime, most of these side streams are choked with little wild iris wildflowers—they tend to grow in bunches, and are actually all connected by their roots.

The wonderful stroll continues, across another pretty good sized side stream, then the trail heads uphill just a little. It levels off and crosses the steep hillside to an SSS at 191.4. There is a neat rock outcrop just below the trail, the forest floor is carpeted with thick mosses and huckleberry bushes, and there is a nice view looking right down on the creek. Then the trail heads on down along a moss-covered trail, and past fern and flower-covered hillsides. Nice big oaks around too.

It swings to the right, away from the creek and runs mostly level, but some uphill. It swings back to the left, rejoining the creek again at 191.8, and comes to a registration box. Just beyond, it heads up a flight of steps, and we bid our wonderful Hilary Hollow good-bye as we cross Hwy. 9. There is somewhat of a parking area here, but no official trailhead. This is 2.7 miles south of the Hwys. 9/10 junction (the store there has gas, groceries and a phone). By the way, you can almost always find water in the creek here all year.

The trail heads into the woods, up a flight of steps (not on the old road to the right), and it heads pretty steeply up. You may notice that the bright blue blazes are joined by some darker ones—these darker ones are put up by the good folks at Pinnacle Mountain State Park, and they will be showing the way from now on. We are still in the Ouachita National Forest for the time being, but will leave it soon.

The trail swings to the left, not quite so steep, across a huckleberry hillside. It eases to the right and passes the last Forest Service MILEPOST, which is #192. The milemarkers from now on for the rest of the trail will be white metal diamonds nailed to trees, with black vinyl numbers stuck on them. These replace plastic ones I had put up many years ago, and they should last a good long while. You will also begin to see signs stating mileages to various spots towards the State Park. Some are correct, and some are not. Refer to the mileages in this text and on the maps for the most accurate readings.

It continues to head uphill a little more, across several rocky drainages. It turns up into the hill and passes an odd "N" tree on the left that is kind of laid down on the ground. The trail levels off, and actually begins to ease on downhill some. Just as it levels off again and things get rocky, we come to the Forest Service boundary at 192.5. There is a sign there that explains the property ownership ahead.

The next six miles are owned by various private concerns, including paper and grass companies. We certainly do appreciate them allowing this trail to cross their lands. Please don't get offended if you see timber practices going on—like clear-cuts. Actually, I think that most of the area along the trail has been cut and won't be disturbed much for a while. Anyway, respect their rights, and enjoy the trail. By the way, you will notice lots of paint on many of the trees. This gets confusing at times, but just be sure to follow the normal BLUE BLAZES.

NOTE: Camping is NOT allowed along the trail for the rest of this section. The next legal place to camp is accessed via a spur trail at 208.4 in Section 10 (and that is the only location in Section 10 to camp).

From the property line, the trail heads back downhill, across a drain or two, past a moss and fern-covered hillside. Lots of huckleberry too. It gets a little rocky here and there, but the trail is in good condition. There are a number of rock steps, each flight leading down into and out of a little drainage. And as the drainages come together they are forming a little creek down and to the left, which we'll cross a few times. This is Pipeline Creek—you'll know why in a minute.

The trail heads downhill steeply, picks up an old road trace that takes us to another drainage, then up a flight of steps, and to our first "Ernst diamond" MILEMARKER, #193. From there the trail runs alongside the creek, then turns and crosses it at 193.1. Right after that, the trail heads up a hill and crosses a dirt road. It continues up the hillside, across a couple of small drains, levels off, then heads back down the hill again. The trail is in real good shape through here.

On the way down it picks up an old road trace and continues steeply down the hill. You will notice some purple paint on trees to the right in this area—this color of paint replaces "posted signs" in Arkansas, and means "Private Property, No Trespassing."

The trail quickly hits bottom, and runs across a flat and intersects with a natural gas pipeline right of way at 193.7—TURN LEFT and follow the level, straight road bed that runs along it. There are a few blazes on the rocks, but not many trees to blaze. Pipeline Creek is just off to the right, and has gotten a lot bigger. It is a year-round water supply. In fact, there is plenty of water on this entire section.

The pipeline, and the trail, cross the creek at 193.8. I found some stepping stones just upstream to hop across on, but this would often be a wet crossing. You can see the bare pipeline here. As the pipeline bends around to the left a little, it passes MILEMARKER #194. There is another straight stretch ahead. There is a neat castle rock type outcrop across the creek to the left, surrounded by young pine trees.

The creek curves back over in our way again at 194.2, and a second dry crossing is ify. The road gets a little rocky now. Just before an apparent third crossing of this creek, the trail leaves the pipeline, DOUBLING BACK TO THE LEFT. It crosses a small drain, starts up the hill on a road trace, and JUST A FEW FEET FURTHER, the trail leaves this road trace TO THE RIGHT, and continues uphill. It quickly levels off along the edge of a pine plantation. This stretch of trail for a while gets pretty grown up in summer with lots of weeds and briars—*hint*—sometimes shorts are not the best things to wear in summer.

Soon the trail comes to the edge of a pine plantation and TURNS LEFT up the hill. It runs along the dividing line between one pine plantation of larger trees and one smaller trees. Just as the trail levels out, it swings to the right and heads downhill, still following the line between the small and the larger trees. It gets kind of soupy through here in the wet season. Nice views.

The trail levels out, then runs up just a tad as the creek swings in close. We pick up another old road trace that skirts the pines on the level, and pass MILEMARKER #195. There is a neat rock outcrop down in the creek here—an SSS. A little ways beyond this, the trail intersects with a gravel road at 195.1 (Duffy Lane)—TURN RIGHT and head down the road towards the pipeline.

Continue on the road and across Pipeline Creek (your third and last crossing of it), then TURN LEFT off of the road soon after the creek crossing and continue downstream on normal trail. Lovely hike through this area with the creek off to your left a little bit. (there used to be a trail bridge across the creek and you may see the skeleton of it downstream, but the new route crossing on the road is much safer).

Before long the trail comes out to the Big Maumelle River at 195.6 (we will follow along this all the way to Hwy. 10). There is a big slab of concrete in the river. Gosh, this would be a wet crossing wouldn't it? Good thing we don't cross it. The trail turns TO THE

RIGHT and heads downstream. The river swings away from it for a while, and the trail gets very grown up with briars and river cane. And wildflowers. Lots of wildflowers.

At 195.8 we come alongside a much slower-moving Maumelle river, and there are a few large cypress trees there—pretty neat for this 'ol hill boy. Lots of "cypress knees" too. The trail, on the other hand, gets to be a mess—it's overgrown with briars and cane. I probably should have mentioned that you shouldn't wear shorts through here. I told you to read each section before you hiked it!

The trail swings away from the river and comes to a deeply-cut side drainage that it goes down into and out of. There was a big log here that I crossed on. It then swings back to the left, still in the thick stuff, then alongside the river again, which is split into two sections. There is an SSS area there of big cypress trees and lazy turtles sunning on the logs. It's real nice trail for a short distance. Then, just as the river comes together, the trail TURNS RIGHT, away from the river—watch for the two blazes on the trees.

It picks up an old road trace and passes MILEMARKER #196. Just beyond the trail leaves the road trace TO THE LEFT, and continues through honeysuckle and cedar trees as plain trail. All of this is on the level. It crosses a couple of small drains. Nice easy, straight trail. It crosses an old road trace, then a spring-like creek (an SSS), another jeep road, and finally intersects with a dirt road at 196.3—TURN LEFT and go along the road.

*There is a highwater bypass upstream if the creek is flooded—it crosses the creek then goes downstream on the other side to the trail.

Just before the road crosses a larger creek ahead—this is Red Bluff Creek—the trail leaves the road TO THE RIGHT and crosses the creek. The trail continues up the other side to the left as plain trail. Much of this area in the bottoms can get confusing, so be sure to stay alert and follow the blue blazes. It is pretty well marked most of the way, so if you don't see a blaze for a while, stop and go back until you do see one, then try to find your way again.

The trail rises up and around a hill a little, and comes to an SSS view down the river at 196.5. This is a wonderful spot on the trail. It is short-lived though, as soon the trail heads steeply down the hill into the bottoms again. There is a fence line here that we'll see a lot of, as the trail follows it. There is a different kind of pine plantation on the right— tall spindly trees that have been recently thinned out.

There is a lot of river cane now along the trail, and a giant oak tree. It crosses a couple of small drains. Many of these don't have too much water in them, but they do often require some imagination to figure out how to get across dry. The trail curves around to the left, following the fence, through a springtime SSS area—the forest floor here was absolutely covered with may apples.

It runs up a hill some, across a flat, then back down again. Up again, through a boulder field, then level past MILEMARKER #197. It crosses a couple of small drains, doing some short up-and-downing, then heads steeply up the hill to the right, then left. It levels off at 197.2

at a wonderful SSS view. You can look right up the river to the hills beyond. There are lots of rock outcrops here too.

Pretty soon, as the trail begins to ease down the hill, there is a new line of purple paint on the left. This is the property line of the WinRock Grass Farm, which we'll be following for a while. Grass is big business down here. You can look across the river and see the vast fields of grass there. The trail crosses another drain or two, and does some up-and-downing. At 197.5 it comes out to a view of a big power-line tower ahead, and a large pond/small lake across the river—TURN RIGHT here and head away from the river and the fence line.

It soon turns back to the left and runs on down into the powerline right-of-way. TURN RIGHT onto a four-wheeler road that runs under the powerlines, cross a small creek, then TURN LEFT off of the road and head up into the woods away from the powerlines. It rises on up the hill, picks up the fence again, and curves up around to the right, past some nice moss-covered boulders. You may see some "Posted" signs through here—as long as you are on the trail, you are OK. Don't worry about them. But do stay on the trail.

It begins to drop on down the hill back to the left, and passes MILEMARKER #198. It continues down the hill following the fence line, then turns away from it, crosses a small creek, heads up the hill on the other side, then quickly levels. It comes to the fence line again at 198.2 and actually goes through it, crossing into the "purple paint" zone (we do have an easement with them for the trail corridor).

The trail rises up just a little, then eases on down, back through the fence line. It runs down the hill, across a small stream, then back up the other side and level again. Just as it begins to drop on down the hill at 198.5, it comes to a cement post that marks the beginning of Central Arkansas Water Property—we will be on this land from now until we get to State Park property at Pinnacle Mountain. (no camping) The trail turns left at the post and continues down the hill towards the river.

It comes alongside the river and is easy walking on the level. At 198.9 there is a huge cypress tree on the left. Impressive! There's beginning to be some cane again as the trail swings away from the river, which is turning to rapids, past an incredible tree off on the right. This thing is massive! Soon the trail rejoins the river, and at MILEMARKER #199 there is an even bigger cypress tree on the trail. An SSS of course, all these big trees. And the area around them is pretty neat in the spring too, with all the wildflowers and mayapples that come up. Spring is nice on just about any part of the trail.

Soon beyond the tree the trail hits a jeep road—TURN LEFT and follow it until it forks, then take the RIGHT FORK (the left fork runs into the river). Stay on this road for a while. It goes through an old field, then a long stretch through mature pines, and next to the muddy, slow-moving river. It leaves the pines behind, then swings away from the river. The road is just a four-wheeler trail now.

The trail goes through a thick area, then to a wood foot bridge across a small stream at 199.5. There is a larger stream that it crosses beyond, without a bridge. The trail winds around through the bottoms until it intersects another jeep road at 199.7—TURN LEFT and follow this road. It comes alongside the river, and then comes to a messy spot. It's kind of confusing, I hope this helps. The road splits—stay TO THE RIGHT and follow the road around this mess, across a small drain, then up a rocky hill. Just as it levels off, leave the road TO THE RIGHT and head uphill for a short distance. It levels out, crosses a tiny stream, then turns left and crosses a road and heads back to the river.

It continues along the river for a while, past a couple of well-used spots, and comes to MILEMARKER #200. The trail runs along the river and across a couple of drains, one on a bridge. Just after, the trail swings to the right, away from the river, then intersects with a four-wheeler trail at 200.2—TURN LEFT onto the trail and cross a little stream. Lots of tall pines. There is another SSS on the river as we come alongside it for a moment—more cypress trees and knees.

The trail swings away from the river and wanders around in the forest for a while, coming back to the river a time or two. All of this is on the level. At 200.6, right when you least expect it, there is a neat sink hole off to the left, about ten feet across. There is a big tree on one side of it, and lots of mosses and ferns. An SSS of course. But the real important thing, is that right at this spot, the trail leaves the four-wheeler trail TO THE RIGHT.

There is a huge double pine tree on the left, then the trail heads out through a swampy area at 200.8 that gets a little soft and soupy. In fact there are lots of wet spots, and try and try as you might, you are bound to get a little wet at some point. My suggestion is to just splash right through the first one and get it over with. There are lots of spongy mosses that I call "tree moss" covering the ground. If you look real close at them, they look just like a miniature forest.

Finally the trail hits some higher ground (just barely), and heads out through the forest, past MILEMARKER #201. Just beyond, it intersects with a jeep road—TURN LEFT and follow the road. It comes alongside a creek, then the road splits—continue STRAIGHT AHEAD on the road and cross the creek. It quickly splits again—continue STRAIGHT AHEAD here too. This is all pretty well blazed. Follow the main road on to another big powerline right-of-way at 201.2. Continue STRAIGHT ACROSS under the lines (leaving the road).

The trail winds around a little and comes to a gravel road at 201.4—TURN LEFT and follow this road across a creek on a concrete pad (often a wet crossing). Soon the road swings to the right up a hill, and the trail leaves the road TO THE LEFT as just plain trail. The beginning of Lake Maumelle becomes visible off to the left, as is the Hwy. 10 bridge across it (OT goes across it). The trail continues through a pine forest as real nice trail, then comes out to Hwy. 10 right at MILEMARKER #202. The trail TURNS LEFT and heads along the highway shoulder towards the bridge over the lake and the rest of the OT. This is the end of Section Nine—only one more to go!

SECTION TEN—20.5 miles
Hwy. 10 to Pinnacle Mountain State Park

Trail Point	Mile Point	Mileage West to East	Mileage East to West
Hwy. 10	202.0	0.0	20.5
Hwy. 113, 2nd cross	204.1	2.1	18.4
Sawdust Pile	206.5	4.5	16.0
Reece's Creek	208.2	6.2	14.3
Campsite Spur	208.4	6.4	14.1
Hwy. 300, 1st cross	211.5	9.5	11.0
Lunsford Corner	212.2	10.2	10.3
Vista	215.2	13.2	7.3
Spillway	219.2	17.2	3.3
Hwy. 300, 3rd cross	219.9	17.9	2.6
Summit Trail Parking	221.2	19.2	1.3
Pinnacle Mountain State Park Visitor Center	222.5	20.5	0.0

Section Ten, the last OT section, begins at the picnic area on the south side of the Hwy. 10 bridge over Lake Maumelle. All of this section of trail but the last two miles are owned by Central Arkansas Water, and is part of the Maumelle River Wildlife Management Area, and is managed by the Arkansas Game & Fish Commission. The last part of the trail is in Pinnacle Mountain State Park. The good folks at the Park manage all of this stretch of the trail. *NO CAMPING is allowed in this entire section except for a spot on private property that is accessed via a spur trail at 208.4.* Quads are Martindale, Fourche, Ferndale (just touches a corner of it) and Pinnacle Mountain.

Since the trail runs around the lake there is always plenty of water. It only crosses a couple of flowing streams though. Please note: **Swimming is not allowed in Lake Maumelle**.

The trail is very easy to hike. It works its way around the north side of the lake, up away from it a little, and on a lot of jeep roads, swings past the end of the lake at the spillway, cruises down Hwy. 300 for a little ways, then enters the State Park, runs along the base of Pinnacle Mountain, and finally climbs on up to the State Park Visitor Center. In the middle third of this hike there are lots and lots of short ups and downs. Lots of them.

 From the picnic area, pick up the trail just across the highway. This is mile 202.0. The trail follows the highway, just down below the guard rail, on out to the bridge. You'll have to climb over the guard rail and cross the bridge—be

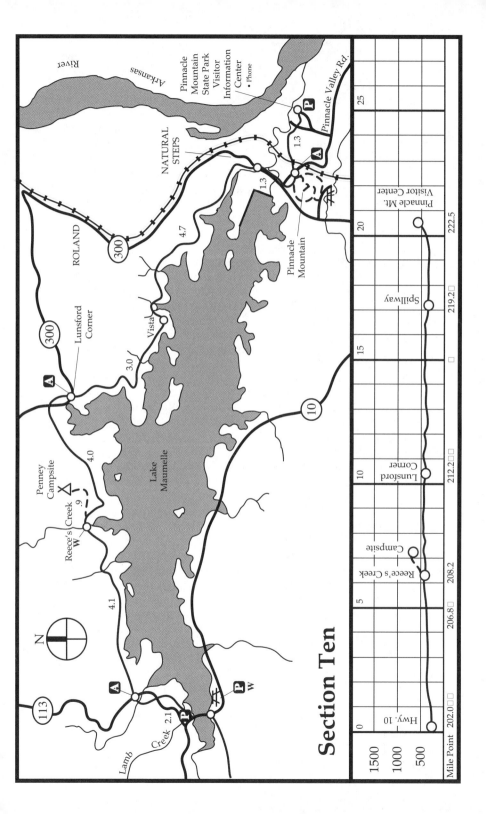

Section Ten

Arkansas River

Pinnacle Mountain State Park
Visitor Information Center
• Phone

NATURAL STEPS

ROLAND

300

Lunsford Corner

300

Penney Campsite

Reece's Creek
W

Lamb Creek 2.1

Lake Maumelle

Vista

Pinnacle Mountain

N

113

4.1

4.0

.9

3.0

4.7

1.3

1.3

A

P

A

P
W

A

10

Pinnacle Valley Rd.

Mile Point																									

Hwy. 10   Reece's Creek   Campsite   Lunsford Corner   Spillway   Pinnacle Mt. Visitor Center

202.0   206.8   208.2   212.2   219.2   222.5

0   5   10   15   20   25

1500
1000
500

careful, because there is usually a lot of traffic. Pretty nice view. Once you get across the bridge, cross the highway (to the lake side) and head towards the woods on the right (look for a brown sign and blue blazes)—the trail goes up into the woods past the sign at 202.4.

It eases up a small hill, across a ridge, then down and across a couple of small creeks. It swings over to the right, across an old road bed, then turns right and crosses another drainage. It wanders around through the woods, gradually up and down some, but mostly on the level. It crosses a wide flat, past MILEMARKER #203. It does some more up-and-downing, makes its way around some private property to the left, across several small drains, then up to and across Hwy. 113 at 203.5.

It climbs to the left up a small hill, then back to the right, and levels off on top. It stays up there for a short while, then drops on down into bottomland. The underbrush gets pretty thick, and the trail comes to a beaver pond area on Young Creek at 203.9, where it crosses three creeks that are feeding it. I had some trouble getting across them dry, and ran into lots of heavy briars when trying to go upstream. After the third crossing the trail turns to the left, climbs up a small bench, and passes MILEMARKER #204. There is a dugout spot on the right here, and the trail swings on over to and across Hwy. 113 again at 204.1.

The trail eases up the hill and swings to the right a little. There is a house just up to the left. We will see several of these along the trail in this area, then again a little later on. It levels out and begins to drop on down the hill past an open coffin on the right at 204.2 (there used to be a coffin beside the trail here—really—now replaced with a gravestone on the left of the trail—be on the lookout for a body). The trail crosses a small creek in the bottom, then a jeep road, and past a trailer off on the left. It heads uphill some more, across a wide ridge, another small drain, then another flat area to a jeep road at 204.7—TURN RIGHT onto this road for just a few feet, then TURN RIGHT again and leave it.

[You will quickly notice that we spend a lot of time in this stretch intersecting with jeep and four-wheeler roads (and describing them here in the text). The trail runs along many of them, most for only short distances. All of this is blazed pretty well, but you do need to be alert for the blazes, especially when you are on one of the roads.]

We are now walking along another type of roadway—an old railroad bed from long ago. I like these things. Good, level, easy hiking. A stroll through history. We will be using this tramway off and on for several miles. It soon passes a small pond on the left, leaving the tramway for a moment. Then it runs off the tramway, on over to a jeep road—TURN RIGHT onto the road. It quickly forks, with the main part going to the right, but we go TO THE LEFT, or straight ahead, on a four-wheeler trail. This soon becomes plain trail, past MILEMARKER #205.

There is lots of thick honeysuckle on either side of the trail. It crosses a couple of small drains, past a wildlife pond, and across another little drain. The trail wanders around some more, and crosses another drain via a big tree root. It rises up just a little, rejoining the tramway for a little ways (it's hard to tell it at this point, since it isn't elevated much). The trail leaves the tramway for a moment to cross a small drain, then back up on it. There are some red private property paint blazes on the trees to the left at 205.6. The tramway sort of disappears, then the trail crosses a couple of road traces and then small drains. It heads uphill just a little, then quickly back down again. Just a short little bump.

It runs level a little, then back up hill again. Most of the trail through this stretch seems to be well used and easy to follow. There are a few views of the lake through the tress here and there. Basically, this is a nice, easy stretch of trail.

The trail gets a little rocky, and the lake comes in pretty close. We are on a high bench looking down on it, and we come to MILE-MARKER #206. It soon drops on down the hill, across a couple of small streams, and gets even closer to the lake. It runs level for a while near the lake, then rises up a rocky stretch, across another drain, and comes to the largest sawdust pile that I've ever seen out in the wild at 206.5. This is a *big* pile, and is all that remains of a sawmill operation that once stood here. The trail curves around the base of the pile, then heads out through the woods again, following the ruts of an old road.

It rises up a little, curving back to the left some, then at 208.6 the trail swings TO THE RIGHT, off of the road ruts for a short distance, then rejoins the old road. Just as the ruts begin to head down the hill, the trail leaves them TO THE LEFT, continuing down the hill, then back up again. There is a line of orange paint along this stretch, just as it tops out it passes MILEMARKER #207. And, of course, it soon begins to head downhill again. It quickly intersects with another jeep road at 207.1—TURN RIGHT and follow this road. A lesser trace comes in from the left, and soon the jeep road curves to the right, and the trail leaves it TO THE LEFT, and continues into the woods as plain trail, crossing a couple of small streams.

It winds back and forth, rises up and levels off along a bench. It passes a concrete post and a rock wall, and then intersects with another jeep road at 207.6—TURN LEFT and follow the road. It rises up a little, then heads downhill a little steeper, and quickly intersects with the tramway, which crosses it from the left as a cut to the right at 207.8—TURN RIGHT onto the tramway, and follow along it. It's piled up pretty good now, and easy to tell apart from the rest of the roads. The trail drops off of it to cross a creek, then gets back up on it.

Soon the tramway flattens out and is joined from the left by the jeep road—continue straight ahead, past MILEMARKER 208. There is a straight stretch, then, just as the road curves to the left, and a rocky stream comes along the right side, the trail leaves TO THE RIGHT. It drops down and crosses the creek, goes alongside the tramway again, then quickly comes to the largest stream on this section at 208.2, which is Reece's Creek, an SSS. Often a wet crossing, but I hear a bridge is in the works. There are lots of neat rounded boulders around.

Once across the creek, the trail climbs back up onto the tramway and continues on. It leaves it once to cross another creek, then again to the right and heads away from it on an old road trace. Soon another jeep road comes in from the left, but we stay on the straight and narrow, across a creek. On the other side, the main jeep road curves up to the left (a lesser one goes to the right), which we stay on, and it gets *very* rocky. Near the top at 208.4, the OT intersects with a spur to the Penney campsite, and leaves this road TO THE RIGHT, and heads out through the woods basically level.

It is a .9 mile climb up to the Penney Campsite along a four-wheeler trail. There are three tent pads and a fire pit there, but no water. Most of the route up and the campsite itself belong to the Penney family who lives nearby, and have graciously allowed hikers to use this spot. THANKS PENNEYS!

From 208.4 the OT runs out across a big flat, across a couple of small drains, then comes to a jeep road intersection. It crosses the main jeep road, but does run along the lesser one which goes TO THE LEFT. Just after that is MILEMARKER #209. And just after that, another jeep road comes in from the left, but the trail continues straight ahead, and drops on down a hill. It goes through a low spot, then heads back up the hill again, where the trail leaves the road TO THE RIGHT, and continues out into the woods. Pretty soon it hits another jeep road—TURN RIGHT and follow this road down through a low area, then uphill some, then level across several small drains. Soon it comes to a "T" intersection at 209.6—TURN LEFT and continue on the jeep road slightly up hill.

It levels off through a cedar thicket and several large mud holes. Soon the trail leaves it TO THE RIGHT, and continues on the level. It wanders around in the low country, past MILEMARKER #210, across a small drain or two. It heads up a pretty good hill, curving back to the left, going up kind of steep for this section. In fact, the biggest climb we've had in quite a while. There is an interesting rock formation up on the right. It tops out at 210.3, picks up a four-wheeler trail, and heads on down the hill, then levels off. There is lots of paint on the trees through here.

Just as the four-wheeler trail makes a sharp turn to the left, the OT leaves it TO THE RIGHT. It heads on out through the woods and drops on down to the bottomland and across a creek at 210.6. It crosses a jeep road, another drain, and then crosses a natural gas pipeline at 210.8—you can see a long ways in both directions here.

The forest floor gets kind of soft and wet for a little while—actually an SSS of thick mosses and lichens. The trail swings to the right some, and pretty soon we pick up our old friend the tramway again, and follow it on past MILEMARKER #211. We leave it at 211.3, run alongside it for a while, then cross it, and eventually rejoin it. Then we come to and across Hwy. 300 at 211.5. There is a huge pine just on the other side. A beautiful tree. An SSS all by itself.

The trail swings to the right, paralleling the highway, and crosses the pipeline again. There's lots of honeysuckle climbing all over the trees. The deer must be happy! The trail swings away from the highway and runs on over to an SSS pond at 211.8. It's a *big* pond. The trail goes along the right side of it, leaving it and heading back out into the woods.

It goes through a swampy area, then passes MILEMARKER #212. There are lots of really tall pine trees through here, and a fat one every now and then. The trail swings away from an even larger pond that can be seen off in the distance to the left, and heads on over to the highway, crossing it again at 212.2. This area is Lundsford Corner.

The trail actually splits for a tiny ways just across the road — take the LEFT TRAIL, which goes on over to pavement, then TURN RIGHT and head down this closed road for about 100 feet, then TURN LEFT off of the road back into the woods again. The other section of trail from the highway goes through a swampy section.

The trail eases on up a hill a little, joins a rocky four-wheeler trail, and gets a little more serious about climbing up. It swings to the left just before the top of the ridge and levels off. It wanders around a little, then begins to drop on down the other side of the ridge. It crosses a little drain, then climbs back uphill again, leveling off just below the top. There are some pretty good views out over the lake from this area. In fact, from here on for a while there will be lots of them, especially during leaf-off. We will be doing a lot more up-and-downing too, more than we've done for quite a while.

It heads up the hill some more, then levels, and passes MILE-MARKER #213. The trail gets rocky in places as it winds around up on the ridgetop. It passes a pile of rocks, turns left and runs downhill some, then levels. The OT TURNS RIGHT and continues along the ridgetop, then drops on down and across a small drain. You will see a lot of the orange painted trees through here again, which is the paper company's property line. The trail heads on uphill, levels out, then drops on back down again. AT 213.6 we intersect with the tramway again—TURN RIGHT and follow it downhill slightly. We soon leave it to the left, and head off up into the woods again.

The trail picks up an old roadway for a little ways, then leaves it TO THE LEFT and heads up a short grade, passing MILEMARKER #214. It quickly levels and swings to the right, then picks up the road ruts again, then quickly leaves them to the right. The trail makes a swooping turn to the right across a small stream, then swings back to the left and heads uphill. There are some good views of the lake through the trees, as the trail heads along the right side of the ridgetop.

It goes through a saddle, then heads on downhill some, past a concrete post, then crosses a small stream and heads back uphill. Up, down. Up, down. Then MILEMARKER #215, right in the stream. Then it heads up a little steeper, back to the left some. Actually it gets quite a bit steeper, and finally levels off on the ridgetop. At 215.2 there is a trail intersection. A short spur goes on out to the right to a vista. It would be pretty nice if they would clear out some of the trees. As it is, you can't see too much. When you can see, you can look across the lake and see Pinnacle Mountain, a place that we've been trying to get to for 215 miles. Yahoo, we're almost there!

The main trail continues STRAIGHT AHEAD. And my pace quickens. The trail heads on down the right side of the ridge at a pretty good clip. It bottoms out across a drain, then heads back up again. Then down. Then level, as the trail swings back to the left. There are lots of tall grasses at 215.5, and it gets a little soupy through here for a short while. Kind of a nice change. I like it. Then the trail crosses a rocky stream, then turns TO THE LEFT and heads up an old road trace along the stream, uphill (there weren't any blazes here for a while when I came through). Soon the trail leaves the roadbed TO THE RIGHT and heads steeply up the hillside, swinging back to the right.

It levels out across the nose of a ridge, then does some more up-and-downing, past MILEMARKER #216 at another drain. From there it heads uphill, and it gets pretty rocky in places. More up-and-downing. Lots of rocks. It gets down almost next to the lake a time or two. Then climbs back up away from it a ways. At 216.6 there is a neat little creek full of rocks. So is most of the hillside. There is *lots* more up-and-downing. You should hear my tape of this section—Up. Down. Up. Down. Up. Down. Up. Down. Past MILEMARKER #217.

Guess what? From there the trail goes down, then back up again. What we are doing is running across a bunch of little finger ridges, and the only way to do it is to go up and over one, then down the other side, then up and over the next one. It keeps things from getting too boring.

At 217.3 we pick up an old road trace, and it swings to the left. Right at a "survey marker" sign, we leave the road TO THE RIGHT, and head pretty steeply up the hill. It levels off, then heads down again, and we intersect with another jeep road and TURN LEFT at 217.5. It eases uphill some, then levels. Soon the trail veers off TO THE RIGHT and leaves the road. We drop on down and pass MILEMARKER #218. The trail does more up-and-downing, across the rocky finger ridges. There are a couple of houses that you may see up to the left on the hillside. Lots of rocks.

There is a neat old twisted pine tree next to the trail at 218.6, and also a faint trail that goes off to the right—the OT heads LEFT and up the hill. More up-and-downing. And a couple of houses up on the hill. We finally come on down out of the hills for good at 218.9 and hit a closed road—TURN LEFT and follow the road which heads slightly uphill. Just as it levels is MILEMARKER # 219. There are big rocks on either side here. Pretty soon the trail leaves the road TO THE RIGHT, and heads on down to the spillway of the lake, which is at 219.2.

The trail comes right out to the edge just below it, an SSS of sorts. And the trail turns to the left there and follows the water downstream. It's a long, straight stretch. Just off of the trail on the left is a no-mans-land. You probably won't see any blazes. At the end of this stretch, the trail veers to the right just a little and heads into the honeysuckle between the water on the right and a paved road on the left. It's a nice little stretch of trail that goes across a wooden bridge at 219.5, then turns to the right. There are several houses off to the left—this is the community of Natural Steps. Civilization! About the first that we've been this close to since Queen Wilhelmina State Park.

Also at that spot is a wonderful SSS view, right down the river, to Pinnacle Mountain, an SSS view (try not to notice the powerlines). I must confess, the day I hiked this stretch, it rained most of the way, and was very foggy. This was the first time that I had seen Pinnacle Mountain from the trail—there was a large grin.

The trail continues alongside the river, past a paved sidewalk that comes in from the left. It soon swings away from the river, then back to it. More good views of Pinnacle. It's a real jungle of honeysuckle. At 219.9 the trail comes out to Hwy. 300—TURN RIGHT and cross the first of two parts of the Maumelle River on the highway bridge. MILEMARKER #220 is tacked onto the first power pole past the far end of the bridge. You should be on the left side of the highway. At first there isn't much shoulder, but there is one before long. Continue walking along the highway toward Pinnacle.

At 220.2 there is a closed paved road TO THE LEFT, which the trail follows through a gate. This is the boundary of Pinnacle Mountain State Park. Just beyond, the trail crosses over the second part of the Maumelle River on the old highway bridge. Hey man, that's a pretty big hiking trail bridge! The pavement soon ends, so follow the shoulder of the main highway on over to Pinnacle Valley Road at 220.5. The trail crosses it and heads into the woods as plain trail once again.

The trail swings over a small drain, then heads up the hill. This is actually the lower flanks of Pinnacle Mountain. It snakes on around across some more little finger ridges and drainages, making its way around Park Staff housing, and up the hill to a trail intersection with a trail that goes around the base of Pinnacle Mountain at 220.6—TURN LEFT to continue on the OT (the base trail goes to the right). There are some neat rounded boulders in the 220.9 area. And soon after is MILE-MARKER #221. From there the trail eases on down the hill, through an open area, into and through the East Summit Trail Parking Area at 221.2. This is a day-use parking area only—vehicles can't be left here overnight.

The OT heads across the parking lot and down across the road. It levels off, crosses a creek, and joins an old road trace TO THE LEFT. It runs alongside a neat swampy area on the left. There is a trail that heads out into it at 221.4—continue STRAIGHT AHEAD up the hill towards the railroad tracks, which the trail soon crosses. It crosses under a big powerline, then picks up another old tramway and runs along it. A nice lovely hike. There are big fields off to the left, and woods up on the right. It curves on around the hill to the right, past a neat rock formation that has a bunch of ferns growing out of it.

Before long the trail leaves the tramway for the last time, to the right, along a road. And soon we intersect with another road—TURN RIGHT and follow this road. It curves on around to the right. The Maumelle River makes one more brief appearance down on the left. Then we go past an open trash dump area on the right. Immediately past this area, the trail leaves the road TO THE RIGHT, across a short aluminum walkway. MILEMARKER #222, the last milemarker on the trail, is located there.

It swings back to the left, then right, across a boulder-strewn stream, an SSS, and up a flight of steps. Then it joins an old road bed for a short stretch, leaving it to the left and continuing up the rocky hillside. It climbs up to and across a paved road, which goes on down to the river for boat access.

The trail heads steeply up the hill, past an SSS rock formation area up and on the left at 222.3. This is the *last* SSS on the Ouachita Trail. Soon the trail levels out and heads to the right, and comes out to the parking area. Turn left and follow the sidewalk to the visitor center, which is at 222.5.

Pinnacle Mtn. State Park is a wonderful park. They stress education to the max. The visitor center exhibits are terrific (they have great t-shirts and other stuff for sale, including all of my guidebooks), and they have an interpretive program of one sort or another going on just about all the time.

Please note—there is **no camping at the park**, and the **gates** to the road leading up to the visitor center are **locked at 10pm** each night. It is OK to leave your car here during an extended hike—be sure to check in at the visitor center and get a registration slip to place on your dash so they don't haul you away. You should park in the main lot at the visitor center.

There is a nice Corps of Engineers campground just a couple of miles away, down along the Arkansas River. They have showers there, which, of course, you will need if you've just hiked the entire Ouachita Trail! By the way, the Park personal here maintain the last 30 miles of the OT, and they would welcome any comments, good or bad, and suggestions that you might have about the trail.

Thanks for staying with me along my hike of the OT. I know we've had our ups and downs, but I hope that you enjoyed the chance to get out and stretch your legs, and I hope you had a *wonderful* time. I know I did.

Come back often…

MY OUACHITA TRAIL HIKE

This is a brief description of my 12-day hike of the OT from end-to-end in late March of 1993. I include it only for your reference, and amusement. I did the hike at a pretty good clip, just because, well, that's the way that I hike. It is hard for me to hike at any other pace. I don't recommend that anyone plan these mileages, or this amount of time to hike the entire trail. Of course, it can be done faster. But it probably should be done at a slower pace. I only saw four other hikers the whole time. Four hikers. In the spring.

Jim Fite dropped me off at Talimena State Park and I began hiking around 11am. I had never hiked this part of the OT before, so it was all new to me. As I always do when I first begin a hike, I took off kind of fast. Then I got to the first hill. Ha ha, 223-miles of this! The clouds hung low. It began to rain a little. I put on my Gore-Tex parka. I was soaked in a few minutes. It had stopped raining, but I was climbing Winding Stair Mountain. It was just cool enough (and the wind was blowing) that I didn't take off that parka for the rest of the day. Must of lost a few pounds.

It got real foggy, and I trudged on through the boulder fields on the north side of the mountain. Each time I thought that I had gotten through the worst of the climb out, there would be another. I wanted to get to the top of the ridge before camping. Darkness stopped me at mile 15.6. I was one tired puppy. There was still mountain left to climb. It was the first day of the hike. My freeze-dried dinner tasted great.

Sometime during the night I formulated a plan that would put me in a room in the Lodge at Queen Wilhelmina on night #3. I was hiking by first light the next day. It was still foggy. I made it to the top of the ridge and had a wonderful hike on to Winding Stair T.H., then more of the same as I scooted on down the south side of the mountain.

It rained only once that day, and I was thrilled to discover that the Forest Service had re-routed the trail so that I only had to cross Big Cedar Creek once instead of three times. I hate creek crossings. By the time I reached the trailhead with the name that I couldn't pronounce (Pashubbe), I was ready to quit day two after 18.7 miles.

I got annoyed early the next day by all of the wilderness signs (my editor says that I can't cuss in this book, so you may never know just exactly how I felt about these), but soon was captivated by the beauty of the Upper Kiamichi Wilderness and forgot about them. There were more crossings of the river than I expected, and I dropped my tape recorder in the river, nearly messing up the rest of the trip. It returned to normal and I pressed on. I wore tennis shoes for all of the river crossings, not stopping to change each time.

The climb up Rich Mountain wasn't all that bad. Then I discovered my "wizard" trees. You've got to understand that us guidebook writers (or at least me) have a lot of time to think about stuff while out there, and odd things often come to mind. Anyway, before long I was propped up in my bed, well fed and clean, watching CNN (sorry, but

I'm hooked). There were 23 messages on my answering machine back home—I've got a long tape. Day three had been a 17.3 mile day.

After a late wake-up call, and a fabulous "Ouachita Trail Breakfast" at the restaurant, I headed out and promptly got hailed on big time. You should hear my tape! Once across the Scenic Drive, the trail became very good and the hiking was terrific. The hail even stopped. I strolled on to Hwy. 71 and stopped for the night, another 16.5 miles under my belt (day four).

I don't remember exactly why, but I got a late start the next day—10am—but made up for it by leaning into the trail, or actually the road, as it is for the first several miles of that section. I nearly ran out of water twice, but managed to find a trickle each time. Lori Creek was wonderful. The climb out was not. The rest of the day was better than the climb, except when I got to an illegal horse trail. I was not a happy camper to see horses using my hiking trail. Once again my editor crossed out my remarks in the text. (The trail has been removed.)

The rest of the day was pretty good, and I ended it near dark at FR #45 after 20.1 miles (day five). I wanted to sleep out under the stars that night, and not set up my tent, but heard a noise in the leaves and decided to put at least a hundredth of an inch of fabric between me and it. When I hike like this, and it gets dark early like it did in March, there isn't a whole lot to do after dinner. So I end up going to bed at 7:30 or 8, which puts me down for something like 10 or more hours. I get up, eat and get ready to hike while it is still dark. Then I wait until I can just barely make out the bark on a nearby tree, then jump up and take off.

Day six was a great day, and I made it the 17.4 miles pretty quick, and stopped for the night on the banks of Harris Creek (FR #149). This was a lovely campsite, and I enjoyed lounging around. I got to visit with genuine hobo that was camped down the river. My freeze-dried dinner wasn't quite as good as his stew. I was in bed by 5 o'clock.

I did the bark thing again on day seven the next morning, and had another good day. It was great to be hiking through so many different mountains instead of the same old ridge all day. And the rushing waters of Story Creek helped rejuvenate me as the miles got long. It was hot when I made that bad climb out from Muddy Creek through the big clear-cut, and it really wore me down. I hit the sack pretty early again at Hwy. 27 after only 16.1 miles.

Day eight was going to be another short day, so I didn't do the bark thing, and ended up getting a late start. The trail was fabulous—smooth and easy hiking. Of course, Sandlick Mountain had a little bit to say about it, but Irons Fork was terrific, and I must admit that I did stop there for a few minutes. And Ariel Falls was a nice surprise. Waterfalls are a dime a dozen on my other trail, the Ozark Highlands, but each one on the OT is a jewel (they are on the OHT also, it's just that we have a treasure chest of them).

I got a glimpse or two of Blue Ouachita Mountain, which made me decide to stop early, rest up, and take it first thing in the morning. I stopped for the night alongside the N. Fork of the Ouachita River after only 17.6 miles (county road 119A).

Let me pause here for a minute and share my menu. I'll be the first to admit that my menu was pretty boring, but it did the job and I didn't go hungry. Here is what I ate, every day (except for the restaurant at Queen Wilhelmina): Breakfast—1 container fruit juice, 1 ramen noodles w/dehydrated vegetables, 1 handful Frosted Mini Wheats; Lunch—actually I had three small lunches everyday, first and third were 1 special energy bar (a Swiss Muesli "Breakbar"), a container of juice and a hand full of Frosted Mini Wheats, and the middle lunch was a beef stick and a handful of Frosted Mini Wheats; Dinner was 1 freeze-dried dinner in a bag, a cup of spiced cider (hot or cold), and you guessed it, a handful of Frosted Mini Wheats for dessert. That was it. My entire menu for twelve days and 223 miles. I like all that stuff.

When I carry a backpack and hike fast all day I get sore, very sore. All over. Even back in 1981, when I walked halfway across the United States for six months (with Jim Rawlins), I still got sore each and every day. The only way that I can keep going is with drugs—I carried aspirin, ibuprofen and acetaminophen on this trip, and alternated between them. Sometimes I even took one of each. About every two hours or so. I was able to keep going.

I didn't look at my watch early on day nine, I just packed up and headed up Blue Ouachita Mountain. The climb was *up*, but not terrible. I find it is usually best to take these climbs first thing in the morning if you can. They always seem a lot taller in the afternoon! Terrific views. Great log shelter. Good trail. It started to rain. Cold, hard blowing rain. I took shelter at the base of one of the antennas up on Ouachita Pinnacle and ate my lunch. I was concerned that it had taken me so long to get there. I wasn't going to make my miles that day. I looked at my watch, and it was only 8:30am! I jumped up and raced down the trail. It stopped raining.

The rest of the miles that day went very well, but I was tired when I made camp near FR #132—I had gone 23.0 miles. After dinner, I watched helplessly as some locals drove up and cut down a giant pine tree near me, then loaded it up on their trailer and sped off. After a long day of hiking, when I get motionless for a while, I can hardly even stand up until morning. I was sad for that tree, and a little embarrassed that I didn't crawl out there and at least protest. I saw *Deliverance*.

It rained that night. I wanted to stay in my tent where it was dry. I was walking by daylight. I had been looking forward to this section the entire hike, since it was the section that I had first hiked back in 1975 when I was in college. The clouds got lower and lower. The wind picked up, and the drops got bigger. I put my tape recorder in a plastic baggie. I wanted so bad to see my beloved Forked Mountain around every turn. Instead all I saw was rain. It was cold too. I didn't realize it at the time, but I was heading for a dangerous situation. I only had a polypro shirt and my Gore-Tex jacket. Plus a thin pair of nylon pants and Helly-Tech rain pants. That was it. Nothing more. The temperature hovered around 38 degrees all day. And the wind was blowing 15–20 miles an hour. Great. Blowing, cold rain, and me with practically nothing on. A simply miserable day.

I was pretty cold, but was able to keep the chill from taking over by walking even harder than I had been. It wasn't looking too good—I had another 20+ miles to do that day. The rain pounded down. I wasn't sure that the bag would protect my valuable (to me) tapes. Then all of a sudden, there it was—Forked Mountain appeared in the mist, and I knew, somehow, that all was well. Oh it continued to rain and blow all day, but I made 22.5 miles by 1:30 in the afternoon.

It's kind of funny. That was probably the coldest that I'd ever been outdoors (and I've spent a lot of days in 20 below out West), and this was also the same stretch of trail that I hiked the longest mileage I'd ever hiked before on. What's going to happen next time I hike this section! I camped near North Fork Pinnacle, and spent the afternoon eating Frosted Mini Wheats, and wondering why I wrote guidebooks.

Day eleven was a different ball game. The sun was out, those proverbial birds were chirping, and I actually saw two other hikers on the trail. I was almost out of the "real" mountains, and into the flatlands and real easy walking. I actually had mixed emotions about that. Ya know, sunshine and easy trail are great. But I wouldn't trade the horrible day that I had just spent in the Flatside Wilderness for ten sunshine days. Really. Think back on your outdoor experiences. Which ones do you have the fondest memories of? For me, it's those days like day ten was, the days where you really have to dig deep down inside, find some character, and go head-to-head with the elements. And you have to win. You *have* to, or it's all over. No game seven. I remember them the most. Those of you who have been there will understand.

Of course, sunshine and easy trail aren't bad, and day eleven was wonderful. Especially the hike through Hilary Hollow. It was as nice as the day before had been miserable. Then it was off of National Forest land and onto private. I always feel much more comfortable on Forest Service land. But it was nice hiking along the river. And those giant cypress trees were just incredible. I stopped for the night after 19.3 miles.

I swear that I didn't recognize it as a coffin. I stashed my measuring wheel in it overnight to keep someone from swiping it. It was eerie listening to the tape as I transcribed my notes—I was talking into the tape recorder when I tried to pull my wheel out of the coffin, and you can hear this weird noise that my wheel made banging against it. It was dark that morning. They told me later that day at the Park that I had just spent the night next to a coffin!

It rained most of day twelve, my last on the OT. Easy trail. Lots of jeep roads. But I liked the sawdust pile, the tramway, the *giant* pine tree, and the view of Pinnacle Mountain that I finally got to see near the end. I was emotional when I walked into the Visitor Center after 18.4 miles that day, and was soaking, dripping wet. My mood quickly changed when I discovered the candy machine.

All in all it had been a terrific hike. I was so happy to have been able to give writing this book as an excuse for getting to spend twelve days hiking the Ouachita Trail. I hope that you can find a reason too…

ABOUT THE AUTHOR

My first footsteps on the Ouachita Trail were way back in 1974 when it was first being built—I used to take students on backpacking trips from an outdoor recreation class I was teaching at the University of Arkansas in Fayetteville. Later I started working on the Ozark Highlands Trail in the Ozarks—building, hiking, taking pictures of and writing about it.

Hiking trails continue to be a part of my daily life as they have been for more then 40 years. I live in a log cabin in the middle of the Buffalo River Wilderness in northwest Arkansas with my lovely bride, Pamela, and our daughter, Amber. I spend a great deal of time out on the trails of our great state, looking for interesting things to photograph, new places to explore, and finding new trails to put into guidebooks.

I am a native and lifelong resident of Arkansas, and while I have traveled quite a bit and worked in many other states on various trail and photography projects, I still find Arkansas the best place of all to live and work. Think I'll stick around a while longer.

You can find info on all of my latest publications and photo workshops, and follow along my daily journal of wilderness life at **www.TimErnst.com**.

Happy Trails to you, and I hope to see ya in the woods!

FRIENDS OF THE OUACHITA TRAIL (FoOT)

Friends of the Ouachita Trail (FoOT) is a non-profit organization of trail users created to provide assistance for the maintenance, enhancement and use of the Ouachita National Recreation Trail. FoOT works as a partner with the USFS/Ouachita National Forest and with Pinnacle Mountain State Park.

FoOT maintains a web site that includes a current trail condition report that is updated frequently. This report is compiled from maintenance reports generated by FoOT volunteers and by other trail users—it is always a good idea to check their site for the latest information about trail conditions, shuttles, and water!

Friends of the Ouachita Trail
P. O. Box 8630, Hot Springs, AR 71910
www.friendsoftheouachita.org

OUACHITA NATIONAL FOREST

Supervisor's Office
P.O. Box 1270
Hot Springs, AR   71902
501–321–5202
(100 Reserve St., 2nd fl.)
www.fs.fed.us/oonf

Choctaw District
HC 63, Box 5184
Hodgen, OK   74939
918–653–2991
(Hwy. 59–270)

Jessieville District
P.O. Box 189
Jessieville, AR   71949
501–984–5313
(Hwy. 7)

Kiamichi District
P.O. Box 577
Talihina, OK   74571
918–567–2326
(Hwy. 271)

Mena District
1603 Hwy. 71N.
Mena, AR   71953
479–394–2382

Oden District
P.O Box 332
Oden, AR   71961
870–326–4322
(Hwy. 88)

Poteau District
P.O. Box 2255
Waldron, AR   72958
479–637–4174
(Hwy. 71)

Winona District
1039 Hwy. 10 North
Perryville, AR   72126
501–889–5176

STATE PARKS

Talimena State Park
P.O. Box 318
Talihina, OK   74571
918–567–2052

Queen Wilhelmina State Park
HC–07, Box 53–A
Mena, AR   71953
479–394–2863

Pinnacle Mountain State Park
11901 Pinnacle Val. Rd.
Little Rock, AR   72223
501–868–5806

TOURIST INFO

Arkansas Parks & Tourism Department
One Capitol Mall
Little Rock, AR   72201
501–682–1191
1–800–NATURAL
www.arkansas.com

Oklahoma Dept. of Tourism & Recreation
2401 N. Lincoln
Okla. City, OK   73105
1–800–652–6552

HUNTING INFO

Arkansas Game & Fish Commission
2 Natural Resources Dr.
Little Rock, AR   72205
501–223–6300
www. www.agfc.com

Oklahoma Dept. of Wildlife Conservation
1801 N. Lincoln
Okla. City, OK   73105
405–521–3981

OUTDOOR STORES

Pack Rat Outdoor Ctr.
209 W. Sunbridge
Fayetteville, AR   72703
479–521–6340
www.packrat.biz

Uncle Sam's Outfitters
1504 N. College
Fayetteville, AR   72703
479–442–0990

Ouachita Outdoor Out.
112 Blackhawk Lane
Hot Springs, AR   71913
501–767–1373
www.ouachitaoutdoors.com

Ozark Outdoor
5514 Kavanaugh Blvd.
Little Rock, AR   72207
501–664–4832

The Woodsman
Central Mall #153
Ft. Smith, AR   72903
479–452–3559

Backwoods
4107 S. Yale
Tulsa, OK   74135
918–664–7850

Backwoods
12325 N. May
Okla. City, OK   73120
405–751–7376

See
www.BikeArkansas.com
for listings of
bike shops in the area

Visit
www.HikeArkansas.com
for lots of other great info
about hiking trails
in Arkansas.

GPS COORDINATES

Here are GPS coordinates for many important points along the trail including trailheads and access areas, road crossings, creek crossings and water holes, and spur trails to shelters. The coordinates are listed in **Lat/Lon Digital Degrees— WGS 84 format**. I find this format to be the easiest to use. It is simple to convert from/into other formats on your GPS unit or computer program if needed (simply change the "units" settings to Digital Degrees—WGS 84).

Location	Mile Point	Lan/Lon Digital Degrees	
Talimena State Park	0.0	34.78360° N	94.95107° W
Military Road Trail	.7	34.78901° N	94.94494° W
Potato Hills Vista Spur	2.4	34.79504° N	94.92369° W
Panorama Vista Spur	5.0	34.77652° N	94.90248° W
FR #6010	5.8	34.77057° N	94.89200° W
Deadman's Gap	8.0	34.77207° N	94.87186° W
Boardstand Trail	8.7	34.77272° N	94.86416° W
Rock Garden Shelter	9.4	34.77312° N	94.86332° W
Cedar Branch	11.2	34.75943° N	94.83161° W
Wildhorse Creek	13.9	34.75735° N	94.79787° W
Spur Trail To Scenic Drive	16.8	34.74644° N	94.76816° W
Holson Valley Vista Shelter	16.8	34.74665° N	94.76793° W
Horsethief/Cedar Lake Trail	18.7	34.74319° N	94.74396° W
Horsethief Springs Spur	19.9	34.73871° N	94.72771° W
Billy Creek West Trail	20.1	34.73811° N	94.72511° W
FR #6014	21.7	34.72666° N	94.70351° W
Billy Creek Trail	22.4	34.72099° N	94.69467° W
Mountain Top Trail	22.9	34.72083° N	94.68941° W
Winding Stair Trailhead	23.7	34.71515° N	94.67894° W
Winding Stairs Shelter/tower	25.0	34.70935° N	94.67742° W
FR #6023/Highwater Bypass	28.3	34.68550° N	94.65911° W
Big Cedar Creek	30.3	34.66801° N	94.65106° W
Big Cedar TH/Hwy. 259	30.5	34.66729° N	94.64945° W
Pashubbe Shelter	34.0	34.66242° N	94.60420° W
Pashubbe Trailhead	34.3	34.66018° N	94.60138° W
Wildlife Pond	34.8	34.66160° N	94.59396° W
Kiamichi River, cross #1	40.9	34.67001° N	94.52146° W
Kiamichi River, cross #8	45.0	34.67776° N	94.48612° W
Arkansas State Line	46.3	34.69338° N	94.45555° W
State Line Shelter	46.4	34.69287°N	94.45198° W
FR# 514	47.8	34.69104° N	94.43048° W
Pioneer Cemetery	49.5	34.68837° N	94.40108° W
Queen Wilhelmina Lodge	51.6	34.68462° N	94.36922° W
Talimena Scenic Dr./Hwy.88	54.1	34.67866° N	94.33644° W
Hwy. 270 TH/Ouachita River	56.7	34.68446° N	94.31776° W

Black Fork Mountain Trail	57.8	34.68884° N	94.30804° W
Black Fork Mtn. Shelter	57.8 (+.1)	34.69062° N	94.31040° W
Eagle Gap/Clear Fork	58.5	34.69046° N	94.30106° W
Creek	67.7	34.67811° N	94.18410° W
Foran Gap/Hwy. 71	68.1	34.68188° N	94.18081° W
Foran Gap Shelter	68.9	34.68635° N	94.17453° W
Tan-a-Hill Gap	74.2	34.68807° N	94.09358° W
Tan-a-Hill Spring	74.2 (+.3)	34.69263° N	94.09575° W
Turner Gap Shelter	79.9	34.67640° N	94.01188° W
FR #76A	85.6	34.66421° N	93.93096° W
FR #76	86.0	34.66217° N	93.92154° W
FR #48	88.2	34.66600° N	93.88609° W
FR #813	90.3	34.66676° N	93.85755° W
Brushy Creek Mtn. Shelter	90.6	34.66873° N	93.85660° W
Brushy Creek Trail	91.4	34.67310° N	93.84158° W
FR #6	94.3	34.68367° N	93.80652° W
Big Brushy CG/Hwy. 270	94.5	34.68511° N	93.81031° W
FR #33	96.0	34.68705° N	93.78909° W
Fiddler Creek Shelter	100.9	34.69205° N	93.72192° W
FR #274 West Cross	101.0	34.69239° N	93.72020° W
Fiddlers Creek/FR #274	101.1	34.69273° N	93.71865° W
Fiddlers Creek East Cross	102.0	34.70333° N	93.71817° W
FR #149	105.5	34.69861° N	93.66865° W
Rainy Creek	105.6	34.70145° N	93.66811° W
Harris Creek	105.8	34.70267° N	93.66580° W
Suck Mountain Shelter	108.6	34.72438° N	93.62868° W
Round Top Trail	114.1	34.70496° N	93.56919° W
Story Creek Shelter/spring	116.7	34.72738° N	93.53960° W
Womble Trail	117.2	34.72639° N	93.53521° W
FR #149/Muddy Creek	118.7	34.74180° N	93.52884° W
Smith Creek	121.1	34.75379° N	93.49933° W
Hwy. 27 Trailhead	121.7	34.75851° N	93.49443° W
John Archer Shelter Spur	122.6	34.75127° N	93.48558° W
FR #148	124.2	34.74806° N	93.46230° W
Uncle Potter Shelter Spur	127.5	34.73798° N	93.42689° W
Irons Fork Creek	128.8	34.73588° N	93.41276° W
FR #78/Muse north cross	133.6	34.73643° N	93.36166° W
Big Branch Shelter Spur	134.0	34.73154° N	93.35998° W
FR #78/Muse south cross	136.1	34.71328° N	93.35627° W
CR #139/Taber Mtn. Rd.	136.9	34.70519° N	93.35130° W
Hwy. 298 Trailhead	138.8	34.68941° N	93.33658° W
Vell Trail Road	139.3	34.69628° N	93.33570° W
Blue Mtn. Shelter Spur	143.2	34.71587° N	93.28975° W
Ouachita Pinnacle Spur	147.0	34.73048° N	93.22663° W
FR #107	147.8	34.73294° N	93.21910° W
Blocker Creek (below trail)	148.0	34.73155° N	93.21135° W
Big Bear Shelter Spur	150.7	34.72492° N	93.18888° W
Pipeline	152.7	34.73473° N	93.16870° W

Old FR #107 (closed)	153.0	34.73675° N	93.16483° W
FR #122/Blakely Creek	157.0	34.75369° N	93.11954° W
Moonshine Shelter Spur	158.4	34.76426° N	93.10525° W
Hunts Loop Trail	159.4	34.76274° N	93.09240° W
Hwy. 7 Trailhead	160.4	34.77402° N	93.08825° W
FR #132	162.3	34.78883° N	93.07386° W
Sugar Creek	163.9	34.80052° N	93.06533° W
FR #153	165.4	34.81088° N	93.06435° W
Oak Mountain Shelter Spur	167.4	34.81850° N	93.03270° W
FR #124 Trailhead	168.8	34.83256° N	93.03225° W
Green Thumb Spring	170.6	34.83444° N	93.00685° W
Grindstone Gap Spur	173.5	34.84251° N	92.97184° W
Creek	175.0	34.84806° N	92.95287° W
Crystal Prong Creek	177.2	34.86126° N	92.93485° W
Flatside Pinnacle TH/FR#94	179.2	34.87464° N	92.91372° W
Flatside Pinnacle Spur	179.4	34.87403° N	92.91113° W
FR #805	179.8	34.87642° N	92.90608° W
Brown Creek Shelter Spur	182.5	34.87448° N	92.86823° W
Brown Creek & TH/FR#805	183.1	34.86872° N	92.86700° W
North Fork Pinnacle Spur	184.8	34.86022° N	92.85551° W
Lake Sylvia Spur	187.3	34.85796° N	92.81922° W
Lake Sylvia Trailhead	187.3 (+.4)	34.86321° N	92.81847° W
FR #152	187.4	34.85760° N	92.81765° W
Chinquapin Gap/Lake Trail	188.7	34.85801° N	92.80432° W
Nancy Mountain Shelter Spur	189.5	34.85196° N	92.79577° W
Hwy. 9 Trailhead	191.8	34.84666° N	92.76480° W
National Forest Boundary	192.5	34.84593° N	92.75565° W
Duffy Lane west cross	195.1	34.86048° N	92.73255° W
Maumelle River	195.6	34.86539° N	92.72599° W
Red Bluff Creek	196.3	34.86424° N	92.71679° W
Duffy Lane east cross	201.4	34.86952° N	92.66225° W
Hwy. 10 west end/picnic	202.0	34.87246° N	92.65356° W
Hwy. 10 east end/TH	202.4	34.87781° N	92.65511° W
Hwy. 113 west cross	203.5	34.88632° N	92.64913° W
Hwy. 113 east cross	204.1	34.89313° N	92.64835° W
Reece's Creek west cross	208.2	34.90541° N	92.59314° W
Penney Campsite Spur	208.4	34.90441° N	92.58946° W
Penney Campsite	208.4 (+.9)	34.90856° N	92.58061° W
Hwy. 300 west cross	211.5	34.91492° N	92.55402° W
Lunsford Corner/Hwy. 300	212.2	34.90785° N	92.55069° W
Lake Maumelle Spillway	219.2	34.86376° N	92.48392° W
Hwy. 300 Bridge	219.9	34.85685° N	92.47966° W
Pinnacle Valley Road	220.5	34.84944° N	92.48557° W
Pinnacle Mtn. Base Trail	220.6	34.84757° N	92.48566° W
East Summit Trailhead	221.2	34.84427° N	92.47871° W
Pinnacle Mountain Office	222.5	34.84460° N	92.46369° W

MAPS LEGEND

————	Ouachita Trail	━━━━	Paved Highway
- - - - -	Other Trails	═══════	Dirt / Gravel Road
○—1.3—○	Mileage Between Points	= = = = =	Jeep Road
P	Trailhead Parking	⑤⑨	Federal Highway
A	Access Point	⑧⑧	State Highway
W	Water Source	③②④	County Road
○~	Spring	[132]	Forest Road
⌂	Trail Shelter	†	Cemetery
△	Campground	?	Visitor Information
⼌	Day Use Area		

Mileage Log For Entire Trail Is On Page 24
GPS coordinates are on page 133

TO ORDER GUIDEBOOKS
VISIT
WWW.TIMERNST.COM

Ouachita Trail

FOR TOURIST AND TRAVEL
INFO SEE
WWW.ARKANSAS.COM
OR CALL
1–800–NATURAL